THE NOVELS, TALES AND SKETCHES OF J. M. BARRIE

Sir *ames* 'bart.

MY LADY NICOTINE
MARGARET OGILVY

PUBLISHED IN
NEW YORK BY
CHARLES SCRIBNER'S
SONS ❧ ❧ 1896 ❧

INTRODUCTION

READERS unknown to me frequently write to ask whether I have really given up smoking, and, whether or not, will I kindly let them know where the Arcadia Mixture is to be got? But I seldom answer either question.

After keeping it locked in my breast for years, however, let me here divulge a dark secret. When I began to write this book I was no smoker. Instead of having given up the practice most reluctantly as described in these untruthful papers, I was smoking my first pipe gingerly, not because I liked it, but because all my friends smoked, and it seemed unsociable not to smoke with them. I had no pleasure in smoking, my highest ambition was to be able to smoke now and again without apparent effort. How I drifted into writing a book on the subject I cannot remember, but the desire to know both sides was doubtless the reason why I wrote as a slave to tobacco. Oddly enough this assumed character obtained an influence over me, I read his views with attention and began to see that there must be something in them. By the time he had clearly demonstrated the folly of smoking I was a convert to the practice.

CONTENTS

MY LADY NICOTINE

CONTENTS

MARGARET OGILVY

MY LADY NICOTINE

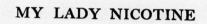

MY LADY NICOTINE

CHAPTER I

MATRIMONY AND SMOKING COMPARED

THE circumstances in which I gave up smoking were these.

I was a mere bachelor, drifting toward what I now see to be a tragic middle age. I had become so accustomed to smoke issuing from my mouth that I felt incomplete without it; indeed the time came when I could refrain from smoking if doing nothing else, but hardly during the hours of toil. To lay aside my pipe was to find myself soon afterwards wandering restlessly round my table. No blind beggar was ever more abjectly led by his dog, or more loth to cut the string.

I am much better without tobacco, and already have difficulty in sympathizing with the man I used to be. Even to call him up, as it were, and regard him without prejudice is a difficult task, for we forget the old selves on whom we have turned

1

our backs as we forget a street that has been re-constructed. Does the freed slave always shiver at the crack of a whip? I fancy not, for I recall but dimly, and without acute suffering, the horrors of my smoking days. There were nights when I woke with a pain at my heart that made me hold my breath. I did not dare move. After perhaps ten minutes of dread, I would shift my position an inch at a time. Less frequently I felt this sting in the daytime, and believed I was dying while my friends were talking to me. I never mentioned these experiences to a human being; indeed, though a medical man was among my companions, I cunningly deceived him on the rare occasions when he questioned me about the amount of to-bacco I was consuming weekly. Often in the dark I not only vowed to give up smoking, but wondered why I cared for it. Next morning I went straight from breakfast to my pipe, without the smallest struggle with myself. Latterly I knew, while resolving to break myself of the habit, that I would be better employed trying to sleep. I had elaborate ways of cheating myself, for it became disagreeable to me to know how many ounces of tobacco I was smoking weekly. Often I smoked cigarettes to reduce the number of my cigars.

On the other hand, if these sharp pains be ex-cepted, I felt quite well. My appetite was as good as it is now, and I worked as cheerfully and certainly harder. To some slight extent, I believe, I experienced the same pains in my boyhood, before I smoked, and I am not an absolute stranger to them yet. They were most frequent in my smoking days, but I have no other reason for charging them to tobacco. Possibly a doctor who smoked himself would have pooh-poohed them. Nevertheless, I have lit my pipe, and then, as I may say, hearkened for them. At the first intimation that they were coming I laid the pipe down and ceased to smoke—until they had passed.

I will not admit that, once sure it was doing me harm, I could not, unaided, have given up tobacco. But I was reluctant to make sure. I should like to say that I left off smoking because I considered it a mean form of slavery, to be condemned for moral as well as physical reasons; but though I see the folly of smoking clearly now, I was blind to it for some months after I had smoked my last pipe. I gave up my most delightful solace, as I regarded it, for no other reason than that the lady who was willing to fling herself away on me said that I must choose between it and her. This deferred our marriage for six months.

I have now come, as those who read will see, to look upon smoking with my wife's eyes. My old bachelor friends complain because I do not allow smoking in the house, but I am always ready to explain my position, and I have not an atom of pity for them. If I cannot smoke here neither shall they. When I visit them in the old Inn they take a poor revenge by blowing rings of smoke almost in my face. This ambition to blow rings is the most ignoble known to man. Once I was a member of a club for smokers, where we practised blowing rings. The most successful got a box of cigars as a prize at the end of the year. Those were days. Often I think wistfully of them. We met in a cosy room off the Strand. How well I can picture it still; time-tables lying everywhere, with which we could light our pipes. Some smoked clays, but for the Arcadia Mixture give me a briar. My briar was the sweetest ever known. It is strange now to recall a time when a pipe seemed to be my best friend.

My present state is so happy that I can only look back with wonder at my hesitation to enter upon it. Our house was taken while I was still arguing that it would be dangerous to break myself of smoking all at once. At that time my ideal of married life was not what it is now, and I remember Jimmy's persuading me to fix on this house because the large room upstairs with the three windows was a smoker's dream. He pictured himself and me there in the summer-time blowing rings, with our coats off and our feet out at the windows; and he said that the closet at the back, looking on to a blank wall, would make a charming drawing-room for my wife. For the moment his enthusiasm carried me away, but I see now how selfish it was, and I have before me the face of Jimmy when he paid us his first visit and found that the closet was not the drawing-room. Jimmy is a fair specimen of a man, not without parts, destroyed by devotion to his pipe. To this day he thinks that mantel-piece vases are meant for holding pipe-lights in. We are almost certain that when he stays with us he smokes in his bed-room — a detestable practice that I cannot permit.

Two cigars a day at ninepence apiece come to £27 7s. 6d. yearly, and four ounces of tobacco a week at nine shillings a pound come to £5 17s. yearly. That makes £33 4s. 6d. When we calculate the yearly expense of tobacco in this way we are naturally taken aback, and our extravagance shocks us the more after we have considered how much more satisfactorily the money might have been spent. With £33 4s. 6d. you can buy new Oriental rugs for the drawing-room, as well as a spring bonnet and a nice dress. These are things that give permanent pleasure, whereas you have no interest in a cigar after flinging away the stump. Judging by myself, I should say that it is want of thought rather than selfishness that makes heavy smokers of so many bachelors. Once a man marries his eyes are opened to many things that he was quite unaware of previously, among them being the delight of adding an article of furniture to the drawing-room every month and having a bedroom in pink and gold, the door of which is always kept locked. If men would only consider that every cigar they smoke would buy part of a new piano-stool in terra-cotta plush, and that for every pound tin of tobacco purchased away goes a vase for growing dead geraniums in, they would surely hesitate. They do not consider, however, until they marry, and then they are forced to it. For my own part, I fail to see why bachelors should be allowed to smoke as much as they like when we are debarred from it.

The very smell of tobacco is abominable, for one cannot get it out of the curtains, and there is little pleasure in existence unless the curtains are all right. As for a cigar after dinner, it only makes you dull and sleepy and disinclined for ladies' society. A far more delightful way of spending the evening is to go straight from dinner to the drawing-room and have a little music. It calms the mind to listen to your wife's niece singing " Oh, that we two were maying." Even if you are not musical, as is the case with me, there is a great deal in the drawing-room to refresh you. There are the Japanese fans on the wall, which are things of beauty, though your artistic taste may not be sufficiently educated to let you know it except by hearsay; and it is pleasant to feel that they were bought with money which, in the foolish old days, would have been squandered on a box of cigars. In like manner every pretty trifle in the room reminds you how much wiser you are now than you used to be. It is even gratifying to stand in summer at the drawing-room window and watch the very cabbies passing with cigars in their mouths. At the same time, if I had the making of the laws I would prohibit people's smoking in the street. If they are married men, they are smoking drawing-room fire-screens and mantel-piece borders for the pink and gold room. If they are bachelors, it is a scandal that bachelors should get the best of everything.

Nothing is more pitiable than the way some men of my acquaintance enslave themselves to to-bacco. Nay, worse, they make an idol of some one particular tobacco. I know a man who con-siders a certain mixture so superior to all others that he will walk three miles for it. Surely every one will admit that this is lamentable. It is not even a good mixture, for I used to try it occasion-ally; and if there is one man in London who knows tobaccos, it is myself. There is only one mixture in London deserving the adjective superb. I will not say where it is to be got, for the result would certainly be that many foolish men would smoke more than ever; but I never knew anything to compare to it. It is deliciously mild yet of full fragrance, and it never burns the tongue. If you try it once you smoke it ever afterwards. It clears the brain and soothes the temper. When I went away for a holiday anywhere I took as much of that exquisite health-giving mixture as I thought would last me the whole time, but I always ran out of it. Then I telegraphed to London for more, and was miserable until it arrived. How I tore the lid off the canister. That is a tobacco to live for. But I am better without it.

Occasionally I feel a little depressed after dinner still, without being able to say why, and if my wife has left me I wander about the room restlessly, like one who misses something. Usually, however, she takes me with her to the drawing-room, and reads aloud her delightfully long home letters or plays soft music to me. If the music be sweet and sad it takes me away to a stair in an Inn, which I climb gaily and shake open a heavy door on the top floor, and turn up the gas. It is a little room I am in once again, and very dusty. A pile of papers and magazines stands as high as a table in the corner furthest from the door. The cane-chair shows the exact shape of Marriot's back. What is left (after lighting the fire) of a framed picture lies on the hearthrug. Gilray walks in uninvited. He has left word that his visitors are to be sent on to me. The room fills. My hand

MATRIMONY AND SMOKING

feels along the mantelpiece for a brown jar. The
jar is between my knees, I fill my pipe. . . .

After a time the music ceases, and my wife puts
her hand on my shoulder. Perhaps I start a little,
and then she says I have been asleep. This is the
book of my dreams.

CHAPTER II

I⊤ was not in my chambers, but three hundred miles further north that I learned to smoke. I think I may say with confidence that a first cigar was never smoked in such circumstances before.

At that time I was a schoolboy, living with my brother who was a man. People mistook our relations, and thought I was his son. They would ask me how my father was, and when he heard of this he scowled at me. Even to this day I look so young that people who remember me as a boy, now think I must be that boy's younger brother. I shall tell presently of a strange mistake of this kind, but at present I am thinking of the evening when my brother's eldest daughter was born — perhaps the most trying evening he and I ever passed together. So far as I knew the affair was very sudden, and I felt sorry for my brother as well as for myself.

We sat together in the study, he on an armchair drawn near the fire and I on the couch. I cannot say now at what time I began to have an inkling

10

that there was something wrong. It came upon me gradually and made me very uncomfortable, though of course I did not show this. I heard people going up and down stairs, but I was not at that time naturally suspicious. Comparatively early in the evening I felt that my brother had something on his mind. As a rule, when we were left together, he yawned or drummed with his fingers on the arm of his chair to show that he did not feel uncomfortable, or I made a pretence of being at ease by playing with the dog or saying that the room was close. Then one of us would rise, remark that he had left his book in the dining-room, and go away to look for it, taking care not to come back till the other had gone. In this crafty way we helped each other. On that occasion, however, he did not adopt any of the usual methods; and though I went up to my bedroom several times and listened through the wall, I heard nothing. At last some one told me not to go upstairs, and I returned to the study, feeling that I now knew the worst. He was still in the armchair, and I again took the couch. I could see by the way he looked at me over his pipe that he was wondering whether I knew anything. I don't think I ever liked my brother better than on that night; and I wanted him to understand that, whatever happened, it would make no difference between us. But the affair upstairs was too delicate to talk of, and all I could do was to try to keep his mind from brooding on it by making him tell me things about politics. This is the kind of man my brother is. He is an astonishing master of facts, and I suppose he never read a book yet, from a Blue Book to a volume of verse, without catching the author in error about something. He reads books for that purpose. As a rule, I avoided argument with him, because he was disappointed if I was right and stormed if I was wrong. It was therefore a dangerous thing to begin on politics, but I thought the circumstances warranted it. To my surprise he answered me in a rambling manner, occasionally breaking off in the middle of a sentence and seeming to listen for something. I tried him on history, and mentioned 1822 as the date of the Battle of Waterloo merely to give him his opportunity. But he let it pass. After that there was silence. By and by he rose from his chair, apparently to leave the room, and then sat down again, as if he had thought better of it. He did this several times, always eyeing me narrowly. Wondering how I could make it easier for him, I took up a book and pretended to read with deep attention, meaning to show him that he could go away if he liked without my noticing it. At last he jumped up, and, looking at me boldly, as if to show that the house was his and he could do what he liked in it, went heavily from the room. As soon as he was gone I laid down my book. I was now in a state of nervous excitement, though outwardly I was quite calm. I took a look at him as he went up the stairs, and noticed that he had slipped off his shoes on the bottom step. All haughtiness had left him now.

In a little while he came back. He found me reading. He lit his pipe and pretended to read too. I shall never forget that my book was " Anne Judge, Spinster," while his was a volume of " Blackwood." Every five minutes his pipe went out, and sometimes the book lay neglected on his knee as he stared at the fire. Then he would go out for five minutes and come back again. It was late now, and I felt that I should like to go to my bedroom and lock myself in. That, however, would have been selfish; so we sat on defiantly. At last he started from his chair, as some one knocked at the door. I heard several people talking, and then loud above their voices a younger one.

When I came to myself, the first thing I thought was that they would ask me to hold it. Then I remembered, with another sinking at the heart, that they might want to call it after me. These, of course, were selfish reflections; but my position was a trying one. The question was, what was the proper thing for me to do? I told myself that my brother might come back at any moment, and all I thought of after that was what I should say to him. I had an idea that I ought to congratulate him, but it seemed a brutal thing to do. I had not made up my mind when I heard him coming down. He was laughing and joking in what seemed to me a flippant kind of way, considering the circumstances. When his hand touched the door I snatched at my book and read as hard as I could. He was swaggering a little as he entered, but the swagger went out of him as soon as his eye fell on me. I fancy he had come down to tell me, and now he did not know how to begin. He walked up and down the room restlessly, looking at me as he walked the one way while I looked at him as he walked the other way. At length he sat down again and took up his book. He did not try to smoke. The silence was something terrible; nothing was to be heard but an occasional cinder falling from the grate. This lasted I should say for twenty minutes, and then he closed his book and flung it on the table. I saw that the game was up, and closed " Anne Judge, Spinster." Then he said, with affected jocularity, " Well, young man, do you know that you are an uncle ? " There was silence again, for I was still trying to think out some appropriate remark. After a time I said, in a weak voice, " Boy or girl ? " " Girl," he answered. Then I thought hard again, and all at once remembered something. "Both doing well?" I whispered. "Yes," he said, sternly. I felt that something great was expected of me, but I could not jump up and wring his hand. I was an uncle. I stretched out my arm toward the cigar-box, and firmly lit my first cigar.

CHAPTER III

THE ARCADIA MIXTURE

DARKNESS comes, and with it the porter to light our stair gas. He vanishes into his box. Already the Inn is so quiet that the tap of a pipe on a windowsill startles all the sparrows in the quadrangle. The men on my stair emerge from their holes. Scrymgeour, in a dressing-gown, pushes open the door of the boudoir on the first floor, and climbs lazily. The sentimental face and the clay with a crack in it are Marriot's. Gilray, who has been rehearsing his part in the new original comedy from the Icelandic, ceases muttering and feels his way along his dark lobby. Jimmy pins a notice on his door "Called away on Business," and crosses to me. Soon we are all in the old room again, Jimmy on the hearthrug, Marriot in the cane-chair; the curtains are pinned together with a pen-nib, and the five of us are smoking the Arcadia Mixture.

Pettigrew will be welcomed if he comes, but he is a married man, and we seldom see him nowadays. Others will be regarded as intruders. If they are smoking common tobaccos, they must

either be allowed to try ours or requested to with-
draw. One need only put his head in at my door
to realize that tobaccos are of two kinds, the Arcadia and others. No one who smokes the Arcadia would ever attempt to describe its delights, for
his pipe would be certain to go out. When he
was at school, Jimmy Moggridge smoked a cane-
chair, and he has since said that from cane to ordinary mixtures was not so noticeable as the
change from ordinary mixtures to the Arcadia. I
ask no one to believe this, for the confirmed
smoker in Arcadia detests arguing with anybody
about anything. Were I anxious to prove
Jimmy's statement, I would merely give you the
only address at which the Arcadia is to be had.
But that I will not do. It would be as rash as
proposing a man with whom I am unacquainted
for my club. You may not be worthy to smoke
the Arcadia Mixture.

Even though I became attached to you, I might
not like to take the responsibility of introducing
you to the Arcadia. This mixture has an extraordinary effect upon character, and probably you
want to remain as you are. Before I discovered
the Arcadia, and communicated it to the other five
— including Pettigrew — we had all distinct in-
dividualities, but now, except in appearance — and
the Arcadia even tells on that — we are as like
as holly-leaves. We have the same habits, the

same ways of looking at things, the same satisfaction in each other. No doubt we are not yet
absolutely alike, indeed I intend to prove this, but
in given circumstances we would probably do the
same thing, and, furthermore, it would be what
other people would not do. Thus when we are
together we are only to be distinguished by our
pipes; but any one of us in the company of persons
who smoke other tobaccos would be considered
highly original. He would be a pigtail in Europe.

If you meet in company a man who has ideas
and is not shy, yet refuses absolutely to be drawn
into talk, you may set him down as one of us.
Among the first effects of the Arcadia is to put an
end to jabber. Gilray had at one time the reputation of being such a brilliant talker that Arcadians locked their doors on him, but now he is a
man who can be invited anywhere. The Arcadia
is entirely responsible for the change. Perhaps I
myself am the most silent of our company, and
hostesses usually think me shy. They ask ladies
to draw me out, and when the ladies find me as
hopeless as a sulky drawer they call me stupid.
The charge may be true, but I do not resent it, for
I smoke the Arcadia Mixture, and am consequently indifferent to abuse.

I willingly gibbet myself to show how reticent
the Arcadia makes us. It happens that I have a
connection with Nottingham, and whenever a man

mentions Nottingham to me, with a certain gleam in his eye, I know that he wants to discuss the lace trade. But it is a curious fact that the aggressive talker constantly mixes up Nottingham and Northampton. "Oh, you know Nottingham," he says interestedly; "and how do you like Labouchere for a member?" Do you think I put him right? Do you imagine me thirsting to tell that Mr. Labouchere is the Christian member for Northampton? Do you suppose me swift to explain that Mr. Broadhurst is one of the Nottingham members and that the "Nottingham lambs" are notorious in the history of political elections? Do you fancy me explaining that he is quite right in saying that Nottingham has a large market-place? Do you see me drawn into half an hour's talk about Robin Hood? That is not my way. I merely reply that we like Mr. Labouchere pretty well. It may be said that I gain nothing by this; that the talker will be as curious about Northampton as he would have been about Nottingham, and that Bradlaugh and Labouchere and boots will serve his turn quite as well as Broadhurst and lace and Robin Hood. But that is not so. Beginning on Northampton in the most confident manner, it suddenly flashes across him that he has mistaken Northampton for Nottingham. "How foolish of me!" he says. I maintain a severe silence. He is annoyed. My experience of talkers tells me that nothing annoys them so much as a blunder of this kind. From the coldly polite way in which I have taken the talker's remarks he discovers the value I put upon them, and after that, if he has a neighbour on the other side, he leaves me alone.

Enough has been said to show that the Arcadian's golden rule is to be careful about what he says. This does not mean that he is to say nothing. As society is at present constituted you are bound to make an occasional remark. But you need not make it rashly. It has been said somewhere that it would be well for talkative persons to count twenty, or to go over the alphabet, before they let fall the observation that trembles on their lips. The non-talker has no taste for such an unintellectual exercise. At the same time he must not hesitate too long, for, of course, it is to his advantage to introduce the subject. He ought to think out a topic of which his neighbour will not be able to make very much. To begin on the fall of snow or the number of tons of turkeys consumed on Christmas Day as stated in the *Daily Telegraph*, is to deserve your fate. If you are at a dinner-party of men only, take your host aside, and in a few well-considered sentences find out from him what kind of men you are to sit between during dinner. Perhaps one of them is an African traveller. A knowledge of this prevents your playing into his hands by remarking that the papers are full of the relief of Emin Pasha. These private inquiries will also save you from talking about Mr. Chamberlain to a neighbour who turns out to be the son of a Birmingham elector. Allow that man his chance, and he will not only give you the Birmingham gossip, but what individual electors said about Mr. Chamberlain to the banker or the tailor, and what the grocer did the moment the poll was declared, with particulars about the antiquity of Birmingham and the fishing to be had in the neighbourhood. What you ought to do is to talk about Emin Pasha to this man, and to the traveller about Mr. Chamberlain, taking care, of course, to speak in a low voice. In that way you may have comparative peace. Everything, however, depends on the calibre of your neighbours. If they agree to look upon you as an honourable antagonist, and so to fight fair, the victory will be to him who deserves it; that is to say, to the craftier man of the two. But talkers, as a rule, do not fight fair. They consider silent men their prey. It will thus be seen that I distinguish between talkers, admitting that some of them are worse than others. The lowest in the social scale is he who stabs you in the back, as it were, instead of crossing swords. If one of the gentlemen introduced to you is of that type, he will not be ashamed to say, " Speaking of Emin Pasha, I wonder if Mr. Chamberlain is interested in the relief expedition. I don't know if I told you that my father" — and there he is, fairly on horseback. It is seldom of any use to tempt him into other channels. Better turn to your traveller and let him describe the different routes to the Egyptian Equatorial Provinces, with his own views thereon. Allow him even to draw a map of Africa with a fork on the table-cloth. A talker of this kind is too full of his subject to insist upon your answering questions, so that he does not trouble you much. It is his own dinner that is spoilt rather than yours. Treat in the same way as the Chamberlain talker the man who sits down beside you and begins, "Remarkable man, Mr. Gladstone."

There was a ventilator in my room, which sometimes said "Crik-Crik!" reminding us that no one had spoken for half an hour. Occasionally, however, we had lapses of speech, when Gilray might tell over again — though not quite as I mean to tell it — the story of his first pipeful of the Arcadia, or Scrymgeour, the travelled man, would give us the list of famous places in Europe where he had smoked. But, as a rule, none of us paid much attention to what the others said, and after the last pipe, the room emptied — unless Marriot insisted on staying behind to bore me with his scruples — by first one and then another putting his pipe into his pocket and walking silently out of the room.

CHAPTER IV

MY PIPES

In a select company of scoffers my briar was known as the Mermaid. The mouthpiece was a cigarette-holder, and months of unwearied practice were required before you found the angle at which the bowl did not drop off.

This brings me to one of the many advantages that my briar had over all other pipes. It has given me a reputation for gallantry, to which without it I fear I could lay no claim. I used to have a passion for repartee, especially in the society of ladies. But it is with me as with many other men of parts whose wit has ever to be fired by a long fuse : my best things strike me as I wend my way home. This embittered my early days , and not till the pride of youth had been tamed could I stop to lay in a stock of repartee on likely subjects the night before. Then my pipe helped me. It was the apparatus that carried me to my prettiest compliment. Having exposed my pipe in some prominent place where it could hardly escape notice, I took measures for insuring a visit from a lady, young, graceful, accomplished. Or I might have it ready for a chance visitor. On her arrival, I conducted her to a seat near my pipe. It is not good to hurry on to the repartee at once; so I talked for a time of the weather, the theatres, the new novel. I kept my eye on her; and by and by she began to look about her. She observed the strange-looking pipe. Now is the critical moment. It is possible that she may pass it by without remark, in which case all is lost; but experience has shown me that four times out of six she touches it in assumed horror, to pass some humorous remark. Off tumbles the bowl. "Oh," she exclaims, "see what I have done! I am so sorry!" I pull myself together. "Madam," I reply calmly and bowing low, "what else was to be expected? You came near my pipe — and it lost its head!" She blushes, but cannot help being pleased; and I set my pipe for the next visitor. By the help of a note-book, of course I guarded myself against paying this very neat compliment to any person more than once. However, after I smoked the Arcadia the desire to pay ladies compliments went from me.

Journeying back into the past, I come to a time when my pipe had a mouthpiece of fine amber. The bowl and the rest of the stem were of briar, but it was a gentlemanly pipe, without silver mountings. Such tobacco I revelled in as may have filled the pouch of Pan as he lay smoking on the mountain-sides. Once I saw a beautiful woman with brown hair, in and out of which the rays of a morning sun played hide-and-seek, that might not unworthily have been compared to it. Beguiled by the exquisite Arcadia, the days and the years passed from me in delicate rings of smoke, and I contentedly watched them sailing to the skies. How continuous was the line of those lovely circles, and how straight. One could have passed an iron rod through them from end to end. But one day I had a harsh awakening. I bit the amber mouthpiece of my pipe through, and life was never the same again.

It is strange how attached we become to old friends, though they be but inanimate objects. The old pipe put aside, I turned to a meerschaum, which had been presented to me years before, with the caution that I must not smoke it unless I wore kid gloves. There was no savour in that pipe for me. I tried another briar, and it made me unhappy. Clays would not keep in with me. It seemed as if they knew I was hankering after the old pipe, and went out in disgust. Then I got a new amber mouthpiece for my first love. In a week I had bitten that through too, and in an over-anxious attempt to file off the ragged edges I broke the screw. Moralists have said that the smoker who has no thought but for his pipe never breaks it; that it is he only who while smoking concentrates his mind on some less worthy object, that sends his teeth through the amber. This may be so; for I am a philosopher, and when working out new theories I may have been careless even of that which inspired them most.

After this second accident nothing went well with me, or with my pipe. I took the mouth-pieces out of other pipes and fixed them on to the Mermaid. In a little while one of them became too wide; another broke as I was screwing it more firmly in. Then the bowl cracked at the rim, and split at the bottom. This was an annoyance until I found out what was wrong and plugged up the fissures with sealing-wax. The wax melted and dropped upon my clothes after a time; but it was easily renewed.

It was now that I had the happy thought of bringing a cigarette-holder to my assistance. But of course one cannot make a pipe-stem out of a cigarette-holder all at once. The thread you wind round the screw has a disappointing way of coming undone; when down falls the bowl, with an escape of sparks. Twisting a piece of paper round the screw is an improvement; but until you have acquired the knack the operation has to be renewed every time you relight your pipe. This involves a sad loss of time, and in my case it afforded a butt for the dull wit of visitors. Other-

wise, I found it satisfactory, and I was soon as-
tonishingly adept at making paper screws. Eventually my briar became as serviceable as formerly,
though not, perhaps, so handsome. I fastened on
the holder with sealing-wax ; and often a week
passed without my having to renew the joint.

It was no easy matter lighting a pipe like mine,
especially when I had no matches. I always
meant to buy a number of boxes ; but somehow I
put off doing it. Occasionally I found a box of
vestas on my mantelpiece, which some caller had
left there by mistake, or sympathizing, perhaps,
with my case ; but they were such a novelty that
I never felt quite at home with them. Generally
I remembered they were there just after my pipe
was lit. When I kept them in mind and looked
forward to using them, they were at the other
side of the room, and it would have been a pity
to get up for them. Besides, the most convenient
medium for lighting one's pipe is paper, after all ;
and if you have not an old envelope in your
pocket, there is probably a photograph standing
on the mantelpiece. It is convenient to have the
magazines lying handy ; or a page from a book —
hand-made paper burns beautifully — will do. To
be sure, there is the lighting of your paper. For this
your lamp is practically useless, standing in the middle of the table, while you are in an easy-chair by the
fireside ; and as for the tape-and-spark contrivance,

it is the introduction of machinery into the softest joys of life. The fire is best. It is near you, and you drop your burning spill into it with a minimum waste of energy. The proper fire for pipes is one in a cheerful blaze. If your spill is carelessly constructed, the flame runs up into your fingers before you know what you are doing; so that it is as well to marry and get your wife to make spills for you. Before you begin to smoke, scatter these about the fireplace. Then you will be able to reach them without rising. The irritating fire is the one that has burned low — when the coals are more than half cinders, and cling to each other in fear of death. With such a fire it is no use attempting to light a pipe all at once. Your better course now is to drop little bits of paper into the likely places in the fire, and have a spill ready to apply to the one that lights first. It is an anxious moment, for they may merely shrivel up sullenly without catching fire, and in that case some men lose their tempers. Bad to lose your temper over your pipe —

No pipe ever really rivalled the briar in my affections, though I can recall a mad month when I fell in love with two little meerschaums, which I christened Romulus and Remus. They lay together in one case in Regent Street, and it was with difficulty that I could pass the shop without going in. Often I took side streets to escape their glances, but at last I asked the price. It startled me, and I hurried home to the briar.

I forget when it was that a sort of compromise struck me. This was that I should present the pipes to my brother as a birthday gift. Did I really mean to do this, or was I only trying to cheat my conscience ? Who can tell ? I hurried again into Regent Street. There they were, more beautiful than ever. I hovered about the shop for quite half an hour that day. My indecision and vacillation were pitiful. Buttoning up my coat, I would rush from the window, only to find myself back again in five minutes. Sometimes I had my hand on the shop-door. Then I tore it away and hurried into Oxford Street. Then I slunk back again. Self whispered "Buy them—for your brother." Conscience said "Go home." At last I braced myself up for a magnificent effort, and jumped into a 'bus bound for London Bridge. This saved me for the time.

I now began to calculate how I could become owner of the meerschaums—prior to despatching them by parcel post to my brother—without paying for them. That was my way of putting it. I calculated that by giving up my daily paper I should save 13s. in six months. After all, why should I take in a daily paper ? To read through columns of public speeches, and police cases, and murders in Paris, is only to squander valuable

29

time. Now, when I left home I promised my father not to waste my time. My father had been very good to me; why, then, should I do that which I had promised him not to do? Then, again, there were the theatres. During the past six months I had spent several pounds on theatres. Was this right? My mother (who has never, I think, been in a theatre) strongly advised me against frequenting such places. I did not take this much to heart at the time. Theatres did not seem to me to be immoral. But, after all, my mother is older than I am; and who am I, to set my views up against hers? By avoiding the theatres for the next six months, I am (already) say, three pounds to the good. I have been frittering away my money, too, on luxuries; and luxuries are effeminate. Thinking the matter over temperately and calmly in that way, I saw that I should be thoughtfully saving money instead of spending it by buying Romulus and Remus, as I already called them. At the same time, I should be gratifying my father and my mother, and leading a higher and a nobler life.

Even then I do not know that I should have bought the pipes until the six months were up, had I not been driven to it by jealousy. On my life, love for a pipe is very like love for a woman, though they say it is not so acute. Many a man thinks there is no haste to propose until he sees a hated rival approaching. Even if he is not in a hurry for the lady himself, he loathes the idea of her giving herself, in a moment of madness, to that other fellow. Rather than allow that, he proposes himself and so insures her happiness. It was so with me. Romulus and Remus were taken from the window to show to a black-bearded swarthy man, whom I suspected of designs upon them the moment he entered the shop. Ah, the agony of waiting until he came out. He was not worthy of them. I never knew how much I loved them until I had nearly lost them. As soon as he was gone I asked if he had priced them and was told that he had. He was to call again to-morrow. I left a deposit of a guinea, hurried home for more money, and that night Romulus and Remus were mine. But I never really loved them as I loved my briar.

CHAPTER V

MY TOBACCO-POUCH

I ONCE knew a lady who said of her husband that he looked nice when sitting with a rug over him. My female relatives seemed to have the same opinion of my tobacco-pouch; for they never saw it, even in my own room, without putting a book or a pamphlet over it. They called it "that thing," and made tongs of their knitting-needles to lift it; and when I indignantly returned it to my pocket they raised their hands to signify that I would not listen to reason. It seemed to come natural to other persons as well as to them to present me with new tobacco-pouches, until I had nearly a score lying neglected in drawers. But I am not the man to desert an old friend that has been with me everywhere and thoroughly knows my ways. Once, indeed, I came near to being unfaithful to my tobacco-pouch, and I mean to tell how; partly as a punishment to myself.

The incident took place several years ago. Gilray and I had set out on a walking tour of the Shakspeare country; but we separated at Strat-

ford, which was to be our starting-point, because
he would not wait for me. I am more of a Shak-
spearian student than Gilray, and Stratford affected
me so much that I passed day after day smoking
reverently at the hotel door; while he, being of
the pure tourist type (not that I would say a word
against Gilray), wanted to rush from one place of
interest to another. He did not understand what
thoughts came to me as I strolled down the Stratford streets; and in the hotel when I lay down on
the sofa he said I was sleeping, though I was really
picturing to myself Shakspeare's boyhood. Gilray
even went the length of arguing that it would not
be a walking tour at all if we never made a start;
so, upon the whole, I was glad when he departed
alone. The next day was a memorable one to me.
In the morning I wrote to my London tobacconist
for more Arcadia. I had quarrelled with both of
the Stratford tobacconists. The one of them, as
soon as he saw my tobacco-pouch, almost compelled me to buy a new one. The second was
even more annoying. I paid with a half-sovereign
for the tobacco I had got from him; but after gazing at the pouch he became suspicious of the coin,
and asked if I could not pay him in silver. An
insult to my pouch I considered an insult to myself; so I returned to those shops no more. The
evening of the day on which I wrote to London
for tobacco brought me a letter from home saying

33

that my sister was seriously ill. I had left her in
good health, so that the news was the more dis-
tressing. Of course I returned home by the first
train. Sitting alone in a dull railway compartment my heart was filled with tenderness, and I
recalled the occasions on which I had carelessly
given her pain. Suddenly I remembered that
more than once she had besought me with tears
in her eyes to fling away my old tobacco-pouch.
She had always said that it was not respectable. In
the bitterness of self-reproach I pulled the pouch
from my pocket, asking myself whether, after all,
the love of a good woman was not a far more
precious possession. Without giving myself time
to hesitate, I stood up and firmly cast my old
pouch out at the window. I saw it fall at the foot
of a fence. The train shot on.

By the time I reached home my sister had been
pronounced out of danger. Of course I was much
relieved to hear it, but at the same time this was a
lesson to me not to act rashly. The retention of
my tobacco-pouch would not have retarded her
recovery, and I could not help picturing my pouch,
my oldest friend in the world, lying at the foot of
that fence. I saw that I had done a wrong in
casting it from me. I had not even the consolation of feeling that if any one found it he would
cherish it, for it was so much damaged that I knew
it could never appeal to a new owner as it appealed

to me. I had intended telling my sister of the sacrifice made for her sake; but after seeing her so much better, I left the room without doing so. There was Arcadia Mixture in the house, but I had not the heart to smoke. I went early to bed, and fell into a troubled sleep, from which I awoke with a shiver. The rain was driving against my window; tapping noisily on it as if calling on me to awake and go back for my tobacco-pouch. It rained far on into the morning, and I lay miserably, seeing nothing before me but a wet fence and a tobacco-pouch among the grass at the foot of it.

On the following afternoon I was again at Stratford. So far as I could remember I had flung away the pouch within a few miles of the station, but I did not look for it until dusk. I felt that the porters had their eyes on me. By crouching along hedges I at last reached the railway a mile or two from the station, and began my search. It may be thought that the chances were against my finding the pouch; but I recovered it without much difficulty. The scene as I flung my old friend out at the window had burned itself into my brain, and I could go to the spot to-day as readily as I went on that occasion. There it was, lying among grass, but not quite in the place where it had fallen. Apparently some navvy had found it, looked at it, and then dropped it. It was half-full of water, and here and there it was sticking together; but I took it up tenderly, and several times on the way back to the station I felt in my pocket to make sure that it was really there.

I have not described the appearance of my pouch, feeling that to be unnecessary. It never I fear, quite recovered from its night in the rain, and as my female relatives refused to touch it I had to sew it together now and then myself. Gilray used to boast of a way of mending a hole in a tobacco-pouch that was better than sewing. You put the two pieces of gutta-percha close together, and then cut them sharply with scissors. This makes them run together, he says, and I believed him until he experimented upon my pouch. However, I did not object to a hole here and there. Wherever I laid that pouch it left a small deposit of tobacco, and thus I could generally get together a pipeful at times when other persons would be destitute. I never told my sister that my pouch was once all but lost, but ever after that, when she complained that I had never even tried to do without it, I smiled tenderly.

CHAPTER VI

MY SMOKING-TABLE

HAD it not been for a bootblack at Charing Cross I should probably never have bought the smoking-table. I had to pass that boy every morning. In vain did I scowl at him, or pass with my head to the side. He always pointed derisively (as I thought) at my boots. Probably my boots were speckless, but that made no difference : he jeered and sneered. I have never hated any one as I loathed that boy, and to escape him I took to going round by the Lowther Arcade. It was here that my eye fell on the smoking-table. In the Lowther Arcade if the attendants catch you looking at any article for a fraction of a second, it is done up in brown paper, you have paid your money, and they have taken down your address before you realize that you don't want anything. In this way I became the owner of my smoking-table, and when I saw it in a brown-paper parcel on my return to my chambers I could not think what it was until I cut the strings. Such a little gem of a table no smoker should be without; and

I am not ashamed to say that I was in love with mine as soon as I had fixed the pieces together. It was of walnut, and consisted mainly of a stalk and two round slabs not much bigger than dinner-plates. There were holes in the centre of these slabs, for the stalk to go through, and the one slab stood two feet from the floor, the other a foot higher. The lower slab was fitted with a walnut tobacco-jar and a pipe-rack, while on the upper slab were exquisite little recesses for cigars, cigarettes, matches, and ashes. These held respectively three cigars, two cigarettes, and four wax vestas. The smoking-table was an ornament to any room; and the first night I had it I raised my eyes from my book to look at it every few minutes. I got all my pipes together and put them in the rack; I filled the jar with tobacco, the recesses with three cigars, two cigarettes, and four matches; and then I thought I would have a smoke. I swept my hand confidently along the mantelpiece, but it did not stop at a pipe. I rose and looked for a pipe. I had half a dozen, but not one was to be seen, none on the mantelpiece, none on the window-sill, none on the hearthrug, none being used as book-markers. I tugged at the bell till William John came in quaking, and then I asked him fiercely what he had done with my pipes. I was so obviously not to be trifled with that William John (as we called him, because some thought his

MY SMOKING-TABLE

name was William, while others thought it was
John) very soon handed me my favourite pipe,
which he found in the rack on the smoking-table.
This incident illustrates one of the very few draw-
backs of smoking-tables. Not being used to them,
you forget about them. William John, however,
took the greatest pride in the table, and whenever
he saw a pipe lying on the rug he pounced upon
it and placed it, like a prisoner, in the rack. He
was also most particular about the three cigars, the
two cigarettes, and the four wax vestas, keeping
them carefully in their proper compartments,
where, unfortunately, I seldom thought of looking for them.

The fatal defect of the smoking-table, however,
was that it was generally rolling about the floor:
the stalk in one corner, the slabs here and there,
the cigars on the rug to be trampled on, the lid of
the tobacco-jar beneath a chair. Every morning
William John had to put the table together.
Sometimes I had knocked it over accidentally. I
would fling a crumpled piece of paper into the
waste-paper basket. It missed the basket but hit
the smoking-table, which went down like a wooden
soldier. When my fire went out, just because I
had taken my eyes off it for a moment, I called it
names and flung the tongs at it. There was a
crash — the smoking-table again. In time I might
have remedied this; but there is one weakness

39

which I could not stand in any smoking-table. A smoking-table ought to be so constructed that from where you are sitting you can stretch out your feet, twist them round the stalk, and so lift the table to the spot where it will be handiest. This my smoking-table would never do. The moment I had it in the air it wanted to stand on its head.

Though I still admired smoking-tables as much as ever, I began to want very much to give this one away. The difficulty was not so much to know whom to give it to as how to tie it up. My brother was the very person, for I owed him a letter, and this, I thought, would do instead. For a month I meant to pack the table up and send it to him; but I always put off doing it, and at last I thought the best plan would be to give it to Scrymgeour, who liked elegant furniture. As a smoker Scrymgeour seemed the very man to appreciate a pretty, useful little table. Besides, all I had to do was to send William John down with it. Scrymgeour was out at the time; but we left it at the side of his fireplace as a pleasant surprise. Next morning, to my indignation, it was back at the side of my fireplace, and in the evening Scrymgeour came and upbraided me for trying, as he most unworthily expressed it, " to palm the thing off on him." He was no sooner gone than I took the table to pieces to send to my brother. I tied the stalk up in brown paper, meaning to get a box for the other parts. William John sent off the stalk, and for some days the other pieces littered the floor. My brother wrote me saying he had received something from me, for which his best thanks; but would I tell him what it was, as it puzzled everybody? This was his impatient way; but I made an effort, and sent off the other pieces to him in a hat-box.

That was a year ago, and since then I have only heard the history of the smoking-table in fragments. My brother liked it immensely; but he thought it was too luxurious for a married man, so he sent it to Reynolds, in Edinburgh. Not knowing Reynolds, I cannot say what his opinion was; but soon afterwards I heard of its being in the possession of Grayson, who was charmed with it, but gave it to Peele because it was hardly in its place in a bachelor's establishment. Later a town man sent it to a country gentleman as just the thing for the country; and it was afterwards in Liverpool as the very thing for a town.

There I thought it was lost, so far as I was concerned. One day, however, Boyd, a friend of mine who lives in Glasgow, came to me for a week, and about six hours afterwards he said that he had a present for me. He brought it into my sitting-room — a bulky parcel — and while he was undoing the cords he told me it was something quite novel: he had bought it in Glasgow the day before. When I saw a walnut leg I started; in another two minutes I was trying to thank Boyd for my own smoking-table. I recognized it by the dents. I was too much the gentleman to insist on an explanation from Boyd; but, though it seems a harsh thing to say, my opinion is that these different persons gave the table away because they wanted to get rid of it. William John has it now.

CHAPTER VII

GILRAY

GILRAY is an actor, whose life I may be said to have strangely influenced, for it was I who brought him and the Arcadia Mixture together. After that his coming to live on our stair was only a matter of rooms being vacant.

We met first in the Merediths' house-boat, the *Tawny Owl*, which was then lying at Molesey. Gilray, as I soon saw, was a man trying to be miserable, and finding it the hardest task in life. It is strange that the philosophers have never hit upon this profound truth. No man ever tried harder to be unhappy than Gilray; but the luck was against him, and he was always forgetting himself. Mark Tapley succeeded in being jolly in adverse circumstances; Gilray failed (on the whole) in being miserable in a delightful house-boat. It is, however, so much more difficult to keep up misery than jollity that I like to think of his attempt as what the dramatic critics call a *succès d'estime*.

The *Tawny Owl* lay on the far side of the island.

43

There were ladies in it; and Gilray's misery was meant to date from the moment when he asked one of them a question, and she said "No." Gilray was strangely unlucky during the whole of his time on board. His evil genius was there (though there was very little room for him), and played sad pranks. Up to the time of his asking the question referred to, Gilray meant to create a pleasant impression by being jolly, and he only succeeded in being as depressing as Jaques. Afterwards he was to be unutterably miserable ; and it was all he could do to keep himself at times from whirling about in waltz tune. But then the nearest boat had a piano on board, and some one was constantly playing dance-music. Gilray had an idea that it would have been the proper thing to leave Molesey when she said "No"; and he would have done so had not the barbel fishing been so good. The barbel fishing was altogether unfortunate—at least Gilray's passion for it was. I have thought — and so sometimes has Gilray — that if it had not been for a barbel she might not have said "No." He was fishing from the house-boat when he asked the question. You know how you fish from a house-boat. The line is flung into the water and the rod laid down on deck. You keep an eye on it. Barbel fishing, in fact, reminds one of the independent sort of man who is quite willing to play host to you, but wishes you clearly to understand

at the same time that he can do without you.
"Glad to see you with us if you have nothing better to do; but please yourself," is what he says to
his friends. This is also the form of invitation to
barbel. Now it happened that she and Gilray were
left alone in the house-boat. It was evening; some
Chinese lanterns had been lit, and Gilray, though
you would not think it to look at him, is romantic.
He cast his line, and, turning to his companion,
asked her the question. From what he has told
me he asked it very properly, and all seemed to
be going well. She turned away her head (which
is said not to be a bad sign), and had begun to
reply when a woful thing happened. The line
stiffened, and there was a whirl of the reel. Who
can withstand that music? You can ask a question at any time, but even at Molesey barbel are
only to be got now and then. Gilray rushed to
his rod and began playing the fish. He called to
his companion to get the landing-net. She did so;
and after playing his barbel for ten minutes, Gilray
landed it. Then he turned to her again, and she
said "No."

Gilray sees now that he made a mistake in not
departing that night by the last train. He over-
estimated his strength. However, we had something to do with his staying on, and he persuaded
himself that he remained just to show her that she
had ruined his life. Once, I believe, he repeated

his question; but in reply she only asked him if he had caught any more barbel. Considering the surprisingly fine weather, the barbel fishing, and the piano on the other boat, Gilray was perhaps as miserable as could reasonably have been expected. Where he ought to have scored best, however, he was most unlucky. She had a hammock swung between two trees, close to the boat, and there she lay holding a novel in her hand. From the hammock she had a fine view of the deck, and this was Gilray's chance. As soon as he saw her comfortably settled, he pulled a long face and climbed on deck. There he walked up and down, trying to look the image of despair. When she made some remark to him, his plan was to show that, though he answered cordially, his cheerfulness was the result of a terrible inward struggle. He did contrive to accomplish this if he was waiting for her observation; but she sometimes took him unawares, starting a subject in which he was interested. Then, forgetting his character, he would talk eagerly or jest with her across the strip of water, until with a start he remembered what he had become. He would seek to recover himself after that; but of course it was too late to create a really lasting impression. Even when she left him alone (watching him, I fear, over the top of her novel) he disappointed himself. For five minutes or so everything would go well: he looked

as dejected as possible; but as he felt he was suc-
ceeding he became so self-satisfied that he began
to strut. A pleased expression crossed his face,
and instead of allowing his head to hang dismally,
he put it well back. Sometimes, when we wanted
to please him, we said he looked as glum as a
mute at a funeral. Even that, however, defeated
his object, for it flattered him so much that he
smiled with gratification.

Gilray made one great sacrifice by giving up
smoking, though not indeed such a sacrifice as
mine, for up to this time he did not know the
Arcadia Mixture. Perhaps the only time he really
did look as miserable as he wished was late at
night when we men sat up for a second last pipe
before turning in. He looked wistfully at us from
a corner. Yet as She had gone to rest, cruel fate
made this of little account. His gloomy face sad-
dened us too, and we tried to entice him to shame
by promising not to mention it to the ladies. He
almost yielded, and showed us that while we
smoked he had been holding his empty briar in
his right hand. For a moment he hesitated, then
said fiercely that he did not care for smoking.
Next night he was shown a novel, the hero of
which had been "refused." Though the lady's
hard-heartedness had a terrible effect on this fine
fellow, he "strode away blowing great clouds into
the air." "Standing there smoking in the moon-

light," the authoress says in her next chapter, "De Courcy was a strangely romantic figure. He looked like a man who had done everything, who had been through the furnace and had not come out of it unscathed." This was precisely what Gilray wanted to look like. Again he hesitated, and then put his pipe in his pocket.

It was now that I approached him with the Arcadia Mixture. I seldom recommend the Arcadia to men whom I do not know intimately lest in the after-years I should find them unworthy of it. But just as Aladdin doubtless rubbed his lamp at times for show, there were occasions when I was ostentatiously liberal. If after trying the Arcadia the lucky smoker to whom I presented it did not start or seize my hand, or otherwise show that something exquisite had come into his life, I at once forgot his name and his existence. I approached Gilray, then, and without a word handed him my pouch, while the others drew nearer. Nothing was to be heard but the water oozing out and in beneath the house-boat. Gilray pushed the tobacco from him, as he might have pushed a bag of diamonds that he mistook for pebbles. I placed it against his arm, and motioned to the others not to look. Then I sat down beside Gilray, and almost smoked into his eyes. Soon the aroma reached him, and rapture struggled into his face. Slowly his fingers fastened on the pouch.

He filled his pipe without knowing what he was doing, and I handed him a lighted spill. He took perhaps three puffs, and then gave me a look of reverence that I know well. It only comes to a man once in all its glory—the first time he tries the Arcadia Mixture—but it never altogether leaves him.

" Where did you get it ? " Gilray whispered, in hoarse delight.

The Arcadia had him for its own.

CHAPTER VIII

MARRIOT

I HAVE hinted that Marriot was our sentimental member. He was seldom sentimental until after midnight, and then only when he and I were alone. Why he should have chosen me as the pail into which to pour his troubles I cannot say. I let him talk on, and when he had ended I showed him plainly that I had been thinking most of the time about something else. Whether Marriot was entirely a humbug or the most conscientious person on our stair readers may decide. He was fond of argument if you did not answer him, and often wanted me to tell him if I thought he was in love: if so, why did I think so; if not, why not? What makes me on reflection fancy that he was sincere is that in his statements he would let his pipe go out.

Of course I cannot give his words, but he would wait till all my other guests had gone, then softly lock the door, and returning to the cane-chair empty himself in some such way as this:—

" I have something I want to talk to you about.

Pass me a spill. Well, it is this. Before I came to your rooms to-night I was cleaning my pipe, when all at once it struck me that I might be in love. This is the kind of shock that pulls a man up and together. My first thought was, If it be love, well and good; I shall go on. As a gentleman I know my duty both to her and to myself. At present, however, I am not certain which she is. In love there are no degrees; of that at least I feel positive. It is a tempestuous surging passion, or it is nothing. The question for me, therefore, is, Is this the beginning of a tempestuous surging passion? But stop; does such a passion have a beginning? Should it not be in flood before we know what we are about? I don't want you to answer.

" One of my difficulties is that I cannot reason from experience. I cannot say to myself, During the spring of 1886, and again in October, 1888, your breast has known the insurgence of a tempestuous passion; do you now note the same symptoms? Have you experienced a sudden sinking at the heart, followed by thrills of exultation? Now I cannot even say that my appetite has fallen off, but I am smoking more than ever, and it is notorious that I experience sudden chills and thrills. Is this passion? No, I am not done; I have only begun.

" In ' As You Like It,' you remember, the love-

symptoms are described at length. But is Rosalind to be taken seriously? Besides, though she
wore boy's clothes she had only the woman's point
of view. I had consulted Stevenson's chapters on
love in his delightful 'Virginibus Puerisque,' and
one of them says, 'Certainly, if I could help it, I
would never marry a wife who wrote.' Then I
noticed a book published after that one, and entitled, 'The New Arabian Nights, by Mr. and
Mrs. Robert Louis Stevenson.' I shut 'Virginibus Puerisque' with a sigh, and put it away.

" But this inquiry need not, I feel confident, lead
to nothing. Negatively I know love; for I do
not require to be told what it is not, and I have
my ideal. Putting my knowledge together and
surveying it dispassionately in the mass, I am inclined to think that this is really love.

" I may lay down as Proposition I. that surging
tempestuous passion comes involuntarily. You
are heart-whole, when, as it were, the gates of your
bosom open, in she sweeps, and the gates close.
So far this is a faithful description of my case.
Whatever it is, it came without any desire or vo-
lition on my part, and it looks as if it meant to
stay. What I ask myself is — first, What is it?
secondly, Where is it? thirdly, Who is it? and
fourthly, What shall I do with it? I have thus
my work cut out for me.

" What is it? I reply that I am stumped at

once, unless I am allowed to fix upon an object definitely and precisely. This, no doubt, is arguing in a circle; but Descartes himself assumed what he was to try to prove. This, then, being permitted, I have chosen my object, and we can now go on again. What is it? Some might evade the difficulty by taking a middle course. You are not, they might say, in love as yet, but you are on the brink of it. The lady is no idol to you at present, but neither is she indifferent. You would not walk four miles in wet weather to get a rose from her; but if she did present you with a rose, you would not wittingly drop it down an area. In short, you have all but lost your heart. To this I reply simply, Love is not a process, it is an event. You may unconsciously be on the brink of it, when all at once the ground gives way beneath you, and in you go. The difference between love and not-love, if I may be allowed the word, being so wide, my inquiry should produce decisive results. On the whole, therefore, and in the absence of direct proof to the contrary, I believe that the passion of love does possess me.

" Where is it? This is the simplest question of the four. It is in the heart. It fills the heart to overflowing, so that if there were one drop more the heart would run over. Love is thus plainly a liquid: which accounts to some extent for its well-recognized habit of surging. Among its effects this may be noted: that it makes you miserable if you be not by the loved one's side. To hold her hand is ecstasy, to press it rapture. The fond lover — as it might be myself — sees his beloved depart on a railway journey with apprehension. He never ceases to remember that engines burst and trains run off the line. In an agony he awaits the telegram that tells him she has reached Shepherd's Bush in safety. When he sees her talking, as if she liked it, to another man, he is torn, he is rent asunder, he is dismembered by jealousy. He walks beneath her window till the policeman sees him home; and when he wakes in the morning, it is to murmur her name to himself until he falls asleep again and is late for the office. Well, do I experience such sensations, or do I not? Is this love, after all? Where are the spills?

" I have been taking for granted that I know who it is. But is this wise? Nothing puzzles me so much as the way some men seem to know, by intuition as it were, which is the woman for whom they have a passion. They take a girl from among their acquaintance, and never seem to understand that they may be taking the wrong one. However, with certain reservations I do not think I go too far in saying that I know who she is. There is one other, indeed, that I have sometimes thought — but it fortunately happens that they are related, so that in any case I cannot go far wrong. After I have seen them again, or at least before I propose, I shall decide definitely on this point.

" We have now advanced as far as Query IV. Now, what is to be done? Let us consider this calmly. In the first place, have I any option in the matter? or is love a hurricane that carries one hither and thither as a bottle is tossed in a chopping sea? I reply that it all depends on myself. Rosalind would say no; that we are without control over love. But Rosalind was a woman. It is probably true that a woman cannot conquer love. Man, being her ideal in the abstract, is irresistible to her in the concrete. But man, being an intellectual creature, can make a magnificent effort and cast love out. Should I think it advisable, I do not question my ability to open the gates of my heart and bid her go. That would be a serious thing for her; and, as man is powerful, so, I think, should he be merciful. She has, no doubt, gained admittance, as it were, furtively; but can I, as a gentleman, send away a weak, confiding woman who loves me simply because she cannot help it? Nay, more, in a pathetic case of this kind, have I not a certain responsibility? Does not her attachment to me give her a claim upon me? She saw me, and love came to her. She looks upon me as the noblest and best of my sex. I do not say I am; it may be that I am not. But I have the child's happiness in my hands; can I trample it beneath my feet? It seems to be my plain duty to take her to me.

"But there are others to consider. For me, would it not be the better part to show her that the greatest happiness of the greatest number should be my first consideration? Certainly there is nothing in a man I despise more than conceit in affairs of this sort. When I hear one of my sex boasting of his 'conquests' I turn from him in disgust. 'Conquest' implies effort; and to lay one's self out for victories over the other sex always reminds me of pigeon-shooting. On the other hand, we must make allowances for our position of advantage. These little ones come into contact with us; they see us, athletic, beautiful, in the hunting-field or at the wicket; they sit beside us at dinner and listen to our brilliant conversation. They have met us, and the mischief is done. Every man — except, perhaps, yourself and Jimmy — knows the names of a few dear girls who have lost their hearts to him — some more, some less. I do not pretend to be in a different position from my neighbours, or in a better one. To some slight extent I may be to blame. But, after all, when a man sees cheeks redden and eyes brighten at his approach, he loses prudence. At the time he does not think what may be the consequence. But the day comes when he sees that he must take

heed what he is about. He communes with himself about the future, and if he be a man of honour
he maps out in his mind the several courses it is
allowed him to follow, and chooses that one which
he may tread with least pain to others. May that
day for introspection come to few as it has come
to me. Love is, indeed, a madness in the brain.
Good-night."

When he finished I would wake up, open the
door for Marriot and light him to his sleeping-
chamber with a spill.

CHAPTER IX

JIMMY

With the exception of myself, Jimmy Moggridge was no doubt the most silent of the company that met so frequently in my rooms. Just as Marriot's eyebrows rose if the cane-chair was not empty when he strode in, Jimmy held that he had a right to the hearthrug, on which he loved to lie prone, his back turned to the company, and his eyes on his pipe. The stem was a long cherry-wood, but the bowl was meerschaum, and Jimmy, as he smoked, lay on the alert, as it were, to see the meerschaum colouring. So one may strain his eyes until he can catch the hour-hand of a watch in action. With tobacco in his pocket Jimmy could refill his pipe without moving, but sometimes he crawled along the hearthrug to let the firelight play more exquisitely on his meerschaum bowl. In time, of course, the Arcadia Mixture made him more and more like the rest of us, but he retained his individuality until he let his bowl fall off. Otherwise he only differed from us in one way. When he saw a match-box he always ex-

58

tracted a few matches and put them dreamily into his pocket. There were times when, with a sharp blow on Jimmy's person, we could doubtless have had him blazing like a chandelier.

Jimmy was a barrister — though this is scarcely worth mentioning — and it had been known to us for years that he made a living by contributing to the *Saturday Review*. How the secret leaked out I cannot say with certainty. Jimmy never forced it upon us, and I cannot remember any paragraphs in the London correspondence of the provincial papers coupling his name with *Saturday* articles. On the other hand, I distinctly recall having to wait one day in his chambers while Jimmy was shaving, and noticing accidentally a long, bulky envelope on his table, with the *Saturday Review's* mystic crest on it. It was addressed to Jimmy, and contained, I concluded, a bundle of proofs. That was so long ago as 1885. If further evidence is required, there is the undoubted fact, to which several of us could take oath, that at Oxford Jimmy was notorious for his sarcastic pen — nearly being sent down, indeed, for the same. Again, there was the certainty that for years Jimmy had been engaged upon literary work of some kind. We had been with him buying the largest-sized scribbling-paper in the market; we had heard him muttering to himself as if in pain; and we had seen him correcting proof-sheets. When we caught him at them he always thrust the proofs into a drawer which he locked by putting his leg on it — for the ordinary lock was broken — and remaining in that position till we had retired. Though he rather shunned the subject as a rule, he admitted to us that the work was journalism and not a sarcastic history of the nineteenth century, on which we felt he would come out strong. Lastly, Jimmy had lost the brightness of his youth, and was become silent and moody, which is well known to be the result of writing satire.

Were it not so notorious that the thousands who write regularly for the *Saturday* have reasons of their own for keeping it dark and merely admitting the impeachment with a nod or a smile, we might have marvelled at Jimmy's reticence. There were, however, moments when he thawed so far as practically to allow (and every one knows what that means) that the *Saturday* was his chief source of income. "Only," he would add, "should you be acquainted with the editor don't mention my contributions to him." From this we saw that Jimmy and the editor had an understanding on the subject, though we were never agreed which of them it was who had sworn the other to secrecy. We were proud of Jimmy's connection with the press, and every week we discussed his latest article. Jimmy never told us, except in a roundabout way, which were his articles; but we knew his style, and it was quite exhilarating to pick out his contributions week by week. We were never baffled, for "Jimmy's touches" were unmistakable; and, "Have you seen Jimmy this week in the *Saturday* on Lewis Morris?" or, "I say, do you think Buchanan knows it was Jimmy who wrote that?" was what we said when we had lit our pipes.

Now I come to the incident that drew from Jimmy his extraordinary statement. I was smoking with him in his rooms one evening, when a clatter at his door was followed by a thud on the floor. I knew as well as Jimmy what had happened. In his pre-*Saturday* days he had no letter-box, only a slit in the door; and through this we used to denounce him on certain occasions when we called and he would not let us in. Lately, however, he had fitted up a letter-box himself, which kept together if you opened the door gently but came clattering to the floor under the weight of heavy letters. The letter to which it had succumbed this evening was quite a package, and could even have been used as a missile. Jimmy snatched it up quickly, evidently knowing the contents by their bulk; and I was just saying to myself, "More proofs from the *Saturday*," when the letter burst at the bottom, and in a moment a score of smaller letters were tumbling about my feet. In vain did Jimmy entreat me to let him

61

gather them up. I helped, and saw, to my bewilderment, that all the letters were addressed in childish hands to "Uncle Jim, care of Editor of *Mothers' Pets.*" It was impossible that Jimmy could have so many nephews and nieces.

Seeing that I had him, Jimmy advanced to the hearthrug as if about to make his statement; then changed his mind, and thrusting a dozen of the letters into my hands, invited me to read. The first letter ran: "Dearest Uncle Jim,—I must tell you about my canary. I love my canary very much. It is a yellow canary, and it sings so sweetly. I keep it in a cage, and it is so tame. Mamma and me wishes you would come and see us and our canary. Dear Uncle Jim, I love you.—Your little friend, Milly (aged four years)." Here is the second: "Dear Uncle Jim,—You will want to know about my blackbird. It sits in a tree and picks up the crumbs on the window, and Thomas wants to shoot it for eating the cherries; but I won't let Thomas shoot it, for it is a nice blackbird, and I have wrote all this myself.— Your loving little Bobby (aged five years)." In another Jacky (aged four and a half) described his parrot; and I have also vaguer recollections of Harry (aged six) on his chaffinch, and Archie (five) on his linnet. "What does it mean?" I demanded of Jimmy, who, while I read, had been smoking savagely. "Don't you see they are in for a prize?" he growled. Then he made his statement.

"I have never," Jimmy said, "contributed to the *Saturday*, nor, indeed, to any well-known paper. That, however, was only because the editors would not meet me half-way. After many disappointments, fortune—whether good or bad I cannot say —introduced me to the editor of *Mothers' Pets*, a weekly journal whose title sufficiently suggests its character. Though you may never have heard of it, *Mothers' Pets* has a wide circulation and is a great property. I was asked to join the staff under the name of 'Uncle Jim,' and did not see my way to refuse. I inaugurated a new feature. Mothers' pets were cordially invited to correspond with me on topics to be suggested week by week, and prizes were to be given for the best letters. This feature has been an enormous success, and I get the most affectionate letters from mothers, consulting me about teething and the like, every week. They say that I am dearer to their children than most real uncles, and they often urge me to go and stay with them. There are lots of kisses awaiting me. I also get similar invitations from the little beasts themselves. Pass the Arcadia."

CHAPTER X

SCRYMGEOUR

SCRYMGEOUR was an artist and a man of means, so proud of his profession that he gave all his pictures fancy prices, and so wealthy that he could have bought them. To him I went when I wanted money — though it must not be thought that I borrowed. In the days of the Arcadia Mixture I had no bank account. As my cheques dribbled in I stuffed them into a torn leather case that was kept together by a piece of twine, and when Want tapped at my chamber door, I drew out the cheque that seemed most willing to come, and exchanged with Scrymgeour. In his detestation of argument Scrymgeour resembled myself, but otherwise we differed as much as men may differ who smoke the Arcadia. He read little, yet surprised us by a smattering of knowledge about all important books that had been out for a few months, until we discovered that he got his information from a friend in India. He had also, I remember, a romantic notion that Africa might be civilized by the Arcadia Mixture. As I shall explain presently, his

64

devotion to the Arcadia very nearly married him against his will; but first I must describe his boudoir.

We always called it Scrymgeour's boudoir after it had ceased to deserve the censure, just as we call Moggridge Jimmy because he was Jimmy to some of us as a boy. Scrymgeour deserted his fine rooms in Bayswater for the Inn some months after the Arcadia Mixture had reconstructed him, but his chambers were the best on our stair, and with the help of a workman from the Japanese Village he converted them into an Oriental dream. Our housekeeper thought little of the rest of us while the boudoir was there to be gazed at, and even William John would not spill the coffee in it. When the boudoir was ready for inspection, Scrymgeour led me to it, and as the door opened I suddenly remembered that my boots were muddy. The ceiling was a great Japanese Christmas card representing the heavens: heavy clouds floated round a pale moon, and with the dusk the stars came out. The walls, instead of being papered, were hung with a soft Japanese cloth, and fantastic figures frolicked round a fireplace that held a bamboo fan. There was no mantelpiece. The room was very small; but, when you wanted a blue velvet desk to write on, you had only to press a spring against the wall; and if you leaned upon the desk the Japanese workmen were ready to make you a new one. There were springs everywhere, shaped liked birds and mice and butterflies; and when you touched one of them something was sure to come out. Blood-coloured curtains separated the room from the alcove where Scrymgeour was to rest by night, and his bed became a bath by simply turning it upside-down. On one side of the bed was a wine-bin, with a ladder running up to it; the door of the sitting-room was a symphony in grey, with shadowy reptiles crawling across the panels; and the floor — dark, mysterious — presented a fanciful picture of the infernal regions. Scrymgeour said hopefully that the place would look cosier after he had his pictures in it; but he stopped me when I began to fill my pipe. He believed, he said, that smoking was not a Japanese custom; and there was no use taking Japanese chambers unless you lived up to them. Here was a revelation. Scrymgeour proposed to live his life in harmony with these rooms. I felt too sad at heart to say much to him then, but, promising to look in again soon, I shook hands with my unhappy friend and went away.

It happened, however, that Scrymgeour had been several times in my rooms before I was able to visit him again. My hand was on his door-bell, when I noticed a figure I thought I knew lounging at the foot of the stair. It was Scrymgeour himself, and he was smoking the Arcadia. We greeted each other languidly on the door-step, Scrymgeour assuring me that " Japan in London " was a grand idea. It gave a zest to life, banishing the poor weary conventionalities of one's surroundings. This was said while we still stood at the door, and I began to wonder why Scrymgeour did not enter his rooms. " A beautiful night! " he said, rapturously. A cruel east wind was blowing. He insisted that evening was the time for thinking, and that east winds brace you up. Would I have a cigar? I would if he asked me inside to smoke it. My friend sighed. " I thought I told you," he said, " that I don't smoke in my chambers. It is n't the thing." Then he explained hesitatingly that he had n't given up smoking. " I come down here," he said, " with my pipe, and walk up and down. I assure you it is quite a new sensation, and I much prefer it to lolling in an easy-chair." The poor fellow shivered as he spoke, and I noticed that his great-coat was tightly buttoned up to the throat. He had a hacking cough and his teeth were chattering. " Let us go in," I said; " I don't want to smoke." He knocked the ashes out of his pipe, and opened his door with an affectation of gaiety.

The room looked somewhat more homelike now, but it was very cold. Scrymgeour had no fire yet. He had been told that the smoke would blacken his moon. Besides, I question if he would have dared to remove the fan from the fireplace without consulting a Japanese authority. He did not even know whether the Japanese burned coal. I missed a number of the articles of furniture that had graced his former rooms. The easels were gone; there were none of the old canvases standing against the wall, and he had exchanged his comfortable, plain old screen for one with lizards crawling over it. "It would never have done," he explained, "to spoil the room with English things, so I got in some more Japanese furniture." I asked him if he had sold his canvases; whereupon he signed to me to follow him to the wine-bin. It was full of them. There were no newspapers lying about; but Scrymgeour hoped to manage to take one in by and by. He was only feeling his way at present, he said. In the dim light shed by a Japanese lamp, I tripped over a rainbow-coloured slipper that tapered to the heel and turned up at the toe. "I wonder you can get into these things," I whispered, for the place depressed me; and he answered, with similar caution, that he couldn't. "I keep them lying about," he said, confidentially, "but after I think nobody is likely to call I put on an old pair of English ones." At this point the housekeeper knocked at the door, and Scrymgeour sprang like an acrobat into a Japanese dressing-gown before he cried "Come in!" As I left I asked him how he felt

now, and he said that he had never been so happy
in his life. But his hand was hot, and he did not
look me in the face.

Nearly a month elapsed before I looked in again.
The unfortunate man had now a Japanese rug
over his legs to keep out the cold, and he was
gazing dejectedly at an outlandish mess which he
called his lunch. He insisted that it was not at all
bad; but it had evidently been on the table some
time when I called, and he had not even tasted it.
He ordered coffee for my benefit, but I do not
care for coffee that has salt in it instead of sugar.
I said that I had merely looked in to ask him to
an early dinner at the club; and it was touching
to see how he grasped at the idea. So complete, however, was his subjection to that terrible
housekeeper, who believed in his fad, that he
dared not send back her dishes untasted. As a
compromise I suggested that he could wrap up
some of the stuff in paper and drop it quietly into
the gutter. We sallied forth, and I found him so
weak that he had to be assisted into a hansom.
He still maintained, however, that Japanese chambers were worth making some sacrifice for; and
when the other Arcadians saw his condition they
had the delicacy not to contradict him. They
thought it was consumption.

If we had not taken Scrymgeour in hand I dare
not think what his craze might have reduced him

to.   A friend asked him into the country for ten days, and of course he was glad to go.   As it happened, my chambers were being repapered at the time, and Scrymgeour gave me permission to occupy his rooms until his return.   The other Arcadians agreed to meet me there nightly, and they were indefatigable in their efforts to put the boudoir to rights.   Jimmy wrote letters to editors (of a most cutting nature) on the moon, breaking the table as he stepped on and off it, and we gave the butterflies to William John.   The reptiles had to crawl off the door, and we made pipelights of the Japanese fans.   Marriot shot the candles at the mice and birds; and Gilray, by improvising an entertainment behind the blood-red curtains, contrived to give them the dilapidated appearance without which there is no real comfort.   In short, the boudoir soon assumed such a homely aspect that Scrymgeour on his return did not recognize it.   When he realized where he was he lit up at once.

CHAPTER XI

HIS WIFE'S CIGARS

THOUGH Pettigrew, who is a much more successful journalist than Jimmy, says pointedly of his
wife that she encourages his smoking instead of
putting an end to it, I happen to know that he
has cupboard skeletons. Pettigrew has been married for years, and frequently boasted of his wife's
interest in smoking, until one night an accident
revealed the true state of matters to me. Late in
the night, when traffic is hushed and the river has
at last a chance of making itself heard, Pettigrew's
window opens cautiously, and he casts something
wrapped in newspaper into the night. The window is then softly closed, and all is again quiet.
At other times Pettigrew steals along the kerbstone, dropping his skeletons one by one. Nevertheless, his cupboard beneath the bookcase is so
crammed that he dreams the lock has given way.
The key is always in his pocket, yet when his
children approach the cupboard he orders them
away, so fearful is he of something happening.
When his wife has retired he sometimes unlocks

the cupboard with nervous hand, when the door bursts gladly open, and the things roll on to the carpet. They are the cigars his wife gives him as birthday presents, on the anniversary of his marriage and at other times, and such a model wife is she that he would do anything for her except smoke them. They are Celebros (Regalia Rothschilds), twelve-and-six the hundred. I discovered Pettigrew's secret one night when, as I was passing his house, a packet of Celebros alighted on my head. I demanded an explanation, and I got it on the promise that I would not mention the matter to the other Arcadians.

"Several years having elapsed," said Pettigrew, "since I pretended to smoke and enjoy my first Celebro, I could not now undeceive my wife — it would be such a blow to her. At the time it could have been done easily. She began by making trial of a few. There were seven of them in an envelope; and I knew at once that she had got them for a shilling. She had heard me saying that eightpence is a sad price to pay for a cigar — I prefer them at tenpence — and a few days afterwards she produced her first Celebros. Each of them had, and has, a gold ribbon round it, bearing the legend, "Non plus ultra." She was shy and timid at that time, and I thought it very brave of her to go into the shop herself and ask for the Celebros (as advertised); so I thanked her warmly.

HIS WIFE'S CIGARS

When she saw me slipping them into my pocket she looked disappointed, and said that she would like to see me smoking one. My reply would have been that I never cared to smoke in the open air, if she had not often seen me do so. Besides, I wanted to please her very much; and if what I did was weak, I have been severely punished for it. The pocket into which I had thrust the Celebros also contained my cigar-case; and with my hand in the pocket I covertly felt for a Villar y Villar and squeezed it into the envelope. This I then drew forth, took out the cigar (as distinguished from the Celebros), and smoked it with unfeigned content. My wife watched me eagerly, asking six or eight times how I liked it. From the way she talked of fine rich bouquet and nutty flavour I gathered that she had been in conversation with the tobacconist, and I told her the cigars were excellent. Yes, they were as choice a brand as I had ever smoked. She clapped her hands joyously at that, and said that if she had not made up her mind never to do so she would tell me what they cost. Next she asked me to guess the price; I answered 80s. a hundred; and then she confessed that she got the seven for a shilling. On our way home she made arch remarks about men who judged cigars simply by their price. I laughed gaily in reply, begging her not to be too hard on me; and I did not even feel uneasy when

73

she remarked that of course I would never buy those horridly expensive Villar y Villars again. When I left her I gave the Celebros to an acquaintance against whom I had long had a grudge (we have not spoken since), but I preserved the envelope as a pretty keepsake. This, you see, happened shortly before our marriage.

" I have had a consignment of Celebros every month or two since then, and, dispose of them quietly as I may, they are accumulating in the cupboard. I despise myself; but my guile was kindly meant at first, and every thoughtful man will see the difficulties in the way of a confession now. Who can say what might happen if I were to fling that cupboard door open in presence of my wife? I smoke less than I used to do; for if I were to buy my cigars by the box I could not get them smuggled into the house. Besides, she would know — I don't say how, I merely make the statement — that I had been buying cigars. So I get half a dozen at a time. Perhaps you will sympathize with me when I say that I have had to abandon my favourite brand. I cannot get Villar y Villars that look like Celebros, and my wife is quicker in those matters than she used to be. One day, for instance, she noticed that the cigars in my case had not the gold ribbon round them, and I almost fancied she became suspicious. I explained that the ribbon was perhaps a little os-

tentatious; but she said it was an intimation of
nutty flavour: and now I take ribbons off the Celebros and put them on the cigars. The boxes in
which the Celebros arrive have a picturesque design on the lid and a good deal of lace frilling
round the edge, and she likes to have a box lying
about. The top layer of that box is cigars in gold
ribbons, placed there by myself, and underneath
are the Celebros. I never get down to the Celebros.

"For a long time my secret was locked in my
breast as carefully as I shall lock my next week's
gift away in the cupboard, if I can find room for
it; but a few of my most intimate friends have an
inkling of it now. When my friends drop in I am
compelled to push the Celebro box towards them,
and if they would simply take a cigar and ask no
questions all would be well; for, as I have said,
there are cigars on the top. But they spoil everything by remarking that they have not seen the
brand before. Should my wife not be present this
is immaterial, for I have long had a reputation for
keeping good cigars. Then I merely remark that
it is a new brand; and they smoke, probably ob-
serving that it reminds them of a Cabana, which is
natural, seeing that it is a Cabana in disguise. If
my wife is present, however, she comes forward
smiling, and remarks, with a fond look in my di-
rection, that they are her birthday present to her

Jack. Then they start back and say they always smoke a pipe. These Celebros were making me a bad name among my friends, so I have given a few of them to understand (I don't care to put it more plainly) that if they will take a cigar from the top layer they will find it all right. One of them, however, has a personal ill-will to me because my wife told his wife that I preferred Celebro cigars at twelve-and-six the hundred to any other. Now he is expected to smoke the same; and he takes his revenge by ostentatiously offering me a Celebro when I call on him."

CHAPTER XII

GILRAY'S FLOWER-POT

I CHARGE Gilray's unreasonableness to his ignoble passion for cigarettes; and the story of his flower-pot has therefore an obvious moral. The want of dignity he displayed about that flower-pot, on his return to London, would have made any one sorry for him. I had my own work to look after, and really could not be tending his chrysanthemum all day. After he came back, however, there was no reasoning with him, and I admit that I never did water his plant, though always intending to do so.

The great mistake was in not leaving the flower-pot in charge of William John. No doubt I readily promised to attend to it, but Gilray deceived me by speaking as if the watering of a plant was the merest pastime. He had to leave London for a short provincial tour, and, as I see now, took advantage of my good nature.

As Gilray had owned his flower-pot for several months, during which time (I take him at his word) he had watered it daily, he must have known he was misleading me. He said that you got into the way of watering a flower-pot regularly just as you wind up your watch. That certainly is not the case. I always wind up my watch, and I never watered the flower-pot. Of course, if I had been living in Gilray's rooms with the thing always before my eyes I might have done so. I proposed to take it into my chambers at the time; but he would not hear of that. Why? How Gilray came by his chrysanthemum I do not inquire; but whether, in the circumstances, he should not have made a clean breast of it to me is another matter. Undoubtedly it was an unusual thing to put a man to the trouble of watering a chrysanthemum daily without giving him its history. My own belief has always been that he got it in exchange for a pair of boots and his old dressing-gown. He hints that it was a present; but, as one who knows him well, I may say that he is the last person a lady would be likely to give a chrysanthemum to. Besides, if he was so proud of the plant he should have stayed at home and watered it himself.

He says that I never meant to water it, which is not only a mistake but unkind. My plan was to run downstairs immediately after dinner every evening and give it a thorough watering. One thing or another, however, came in the way. I often remembered about the chrysanthemum while I was in the office; but even Gilray could hardly have expected me to ask leave of absence merely to run home and water his plant. You must draw the line somewhere, even in a Government office. When I reached home I was tired, inclined to take things easily, and not at all in a proper condition for watering flower-pots. Then Arcadians would drop in. I put it to any sensible man or woman, could I have been expected to give up my friends for the sake of a chrysanthemum? Again, it was my custom of an evening, if not disturbed, to retire with my pipe into my cane-chair, and there pass the hours communing with great minds, or when the mood was on me, trifling with a novel. Often when I was in the middle of a chapter Gilray's flower-pot stood up before my eyes crying for water. He does not believe this, but it is the solemn truth. At those moments it was touch-and-go whether I watered his chrysanthemum or not. Where I lost myself was in not hurrying to his rooms at once with a tumbler. I said to myself that I would go when I had finished my pipe; but by that time the flower-pot had escaped my memory. This may have been weakness; all I know is that I should have saved myself much annoyance if I had risen and watered the chrysanthemum there and then. But would it not have been rather hard on me to have had to forsake my books for the sake of Gilray's flowers and flower-pots, and plants and things? What right has a man to go and make a garden of his chambers?

All the three weeks he was away, Gilray kept pestering me with letters about his chrysanthemum. He seemed to have no faith in me — a detestable thing in a man who calls himself your friend. I had promised to water his flower-pot; and between friends a promise is surely sufficient. It is not so, however, when Gilray is one of them. I soon hated the sight of my name in his handwriting. It was not as if he had said outright that he wrote entirely to know whether I was watering his plant. His references to it were introduced with all the appearance of after-thoughts. Often they took the form of postscripts: "By the way, are you watering my chrysanthemum?" or, "The chrysanthemum ought to be a beauty by this time;" or, "You must be quite an adept now at watering plants." Gilray declares now that, in answer to one of these ingenious epistles, I wrote to him saying that I "had just been watering his chrysanthemum." My belief is that I did no such thing; or, if I did, I meant to water it as soon as I had finished my letter. (He has never been able to bring this home to me, he says, because he burned my correspondence. As if a business man would destroy such a letter.) It was yet more annoying when Gilray took to post-cards. To hear the postman's knock and then discover, when you are expecting an important communication, that it is only a post-card about a flower-pot — that is really too bad. And then I consider that some of the post-cards bordered upon insult. One of them said, "What about chrysanthemum? — reply at once." This was just like Gilray's overbearing way; but I answered politely and (so far as I knew) truthfully, "Chrysanthemum all right."

Knowing that there was no explaining things to Gilray, I redoubled my exertions to water his flower-pot as the day for his return drew near. Once, indeed, when I rang for water, I could not for the life of me remember what I wanted it for when it was brought. Had I had any forethought I should have let the tumbler stand just as it was to show it to Gilray on his return. But, unfortunately, William John had misunderstood what I wanted the water for, and put a decanter down beside it. Another time I was actually on the stair rushing to Gilray's door, when I met the housekeeper and, stopping to talk to her, lost my opportunity again. To show how honestly anxious I was to fulfil my promise, I need only add that I was several times awakened in the watches of the night by a haunting consciousness that I had forgotten to water Gilray's flower-pot. On these occasions I spared no trouble to remember again in the morning. I reached out of bed to a chair and turned it upside down, so that the sight of it when I rose might remind me that I had something to do. With the same object I crossed the tongs and poker on the floor. Gilray maintains that instead of playing "fool's tricks" like these ("fool's tricks!") I should have got up and gone at once to his rooms with my water-bottle. What? and disturbed my neighbours? Besides, could I reasonably be expected to risk catching my death of cold for the sake of a wretched chrysanthemum? One reads of men doing such things for young ladies who seek lilies in dangerous ponds or edelweiss on overhanging cliffs. But Gilray was not my sweetheart, nor, I feel certain, any other person's.

I come now to the day prior to Gilray's return. I had just reached the office when I remembered about the chrysanthemum. It was my last chance. If I watered it once I should be in a position to state that, whatever condition it might be in, I had certainly been watering it. I jumped into a hansom, told the cabby to drive to the Inn, and twenty minutes afterwards had one hand on Gilray's door, while the other held the largest water-can in the house. Opening the door I rushed in. The can nearly fell from my hand. There was no flower-pot. I rang the bell. "Mr. Gilray's chrysanthemum!" I cried. What do you think William John said? He coolly told me that the plant was dead and had been flung out days ago. I went to the theatre that night to keep myself from thinking. All next day I contrived to remain out of Gilray's sight. When we met he was stiff and polite. He did not say a word about the chrysanthemum for a week, and then it all came out with a rush. I let him talk. With the servants flinging out the flower-pots faster than I could water them, what more could I have done? A coolness between us was inevitable. This I regretted, but my mind was made up on one point: I would never do Gilray a favour again.

CHAPTER XIII

THE GRANDEST SCENE IN HISTORY

THOUGH Scrymgeour only painted in water-colours, I think — I never looked at his pictures — he had one superb idea, which we often advised him to carry out. When he first mentioned it the room became comparatively animated, so much struck were we all, and we entreated him to retire to Stratford for a few months before beginning the picture. His idea was to paint Shakspeare smoking his first pipe of the Arcadia Mixture.

Many hundreds of volumes have been written about the glories of the Elizabethan age, the sublime period in our history. Then were Englishmen on fire to do immortal deeds. High aims and noble ambitions became their birthright. There was nothing they could not or would not do for England. Sailors put a girdle round the world. Every captain had a general's capacity, every fighting-man could have been a captain. All the women, from the Queen downwards, were heroines. Lofty statesmanship guided the conduct of affairs, a sublime philosophy was in the air.

THE GRANDEST SCENE IN HISTORY

The period of great deeds was also the period of our richest literature. London was swarming with poetic geniuses. Immortal dramatists wandered in couples between stage-doors and taverns.

All this has been said many times, and we read these glowing outbursts about the Elizabethan age as if to the beating of a drum. But why was this period riper for magnificent deeds and noble literature than any other in English history? We all know how the thinkers, historians, and critics of yesterday and to-day answer that question; but our hearts and brains tell us that they are astray. By an amazing oversight they have said nothing of the Influence of Tobacco. The Elizabethan age might be better named the beginning of the smoking era. No unprejudiced person who has given thought to the subject can question the propriety of dividing our history into two periods — the pre-smoking and the smoking. When Raleigh, in honour of whom England should have changed its name, introduced tobacco into this country, the glorious Elizabethan age began. I am aware that those hateful persons called Original Researchers now maintain that Raleigh was not the man; but to them I turn a deaf ear. I know, I feel, that with the introduction of tobacco England woke up from a long sleep. Suddenly a new zest had been given to life. The glory of existence became a thing to speak of. Men who had hitherto only concerned themselves with the narrow things of home put a pipe into their mouths and became philosophers. Poets and dramatists smoked until all ignoble ideas were driven from them, and into their place rushed such high thoughts as the world had not known before. Petty jealousies no longer had hold of statesmen, who smoked, and agreed to work together for the public weal. Soldiers and sailors felt when engaged with a foreign foe, that they were fighting for their pipes. The whole country was stirred by the ambition to live up to tobacco. Every one, in short, had now a lofty ideal constantly before him. Two stories of the period, never properly told hitherto, illustrate this. We all know that Gabriel Harvey and Spenser lay in bed discussing English poetry and the forms it ought to take. This was when tobacco was only known to a select few, of whom Spenser (the friend of Raleigh) was doubtless one. That the two friends smoked in bed I cannot doubt. Many poets have done the same thing since. Then there is the beautiful Armada story. In a famous Armada picture the English sailors are represented smoking; which makes it all the more surprising that the story to which I refer has come down to us in an incorrect form. According to the historians, when the Armada hove in sight the English captains were playing at bowls. Instead of rushing off to their ships on receipt of the

news, they observed, " Let us first finish our game."
I cannot believe that this is what they said. My
conviction is that what was really said was, " Let
us first finish our pipes " — surely a far more im-
pressive and memorable remark.

This afternoon Marlowe's " Jew of Malta " was
produced for the first time; and of the two men
who have just emerged from the Blackfriars Theatre one is the creator of Barabas. A marvel to
all the " piperly make-plaies and make-bates,"
save one, is " famous Ned Alleyn "; for when
money comes to him he does not drink till it be
done, and already he is laying by to confound the
ecclesiastics, who say hard things of him, by found-
ing Dulwich College. " Not Roscius nor Æsope,"
said Tom Nash, who was probably in need of a
crown at the time, " ever performed more in action." A good fellow he is withal; for it is Ned
who gives the supper to night at the " Globe " in
honour of the new piece, if he can get his friends
together. The actor-manager shakes his head, for
Marlowe, who was to meet him here, must have
been seduced. into a tavern by the way; but his
companion, Robin Greene, is only wondering if
that is a bailiff at the corner. Robin of the " ruf-
fianly haire," *utriusque academiæ in artibus magister*,
is nearing the end of his tether, and might call to-
night at Shoemaker Islam's house near Dowgate,
to tell a certain " bigge, fat, lusty wench " to pre-

pare his last bed and buy a garland of bays. Ned must to the sign of the " Saba " in Gracious Street, where Burbage and " honest gamesom Armin " are sure to be found; but Greene durst not show himself in the street without Cutting Ball and other choice ruffians as a body-guard. Ned is content to leave him behind; for Robin has refused to be of the company to-night if that " upstart Will " is invited too, and the actor is fond of Will. There is no more useful man in the theatre, he has said to " Signior Kempino " this very day, for touching up old plays; and Will is a plodding young fellow, too, if not over brilliant.

Ned Alleyn goes from tavern to tavern, picking out his men. There is an alehouse in Seacoal Lane — the same where lady-like George Peele was found by the barber, who had subscribed an hour before for his decent burial, " all alone with a peck of oysters " — and here Ned is detained an unconscionable time. Just as he is leaving with Kempe and Cowley, Armin and Will Shakspeare burst in with a cry for wine. It is Armin who gives the orders, but his companion pays. They spy Alleyn, and Armin must tell his news. He is the bearer of a challenge from some merry souls at the " Saba " to the actor-manager; and Ned Alleyn turns white and red when he hears it. Then he laughs a confident laugh, and accepts the bet. Some theatre-goers, flushed with wine, have dared him to attempt certain parts in which Bentley and Knell vastly please them. Ned is incredulous that men should be so willing to fling away their money; yet here is Will a witness, and Burbage is staying on at the "Saba" not to let the challengers escape.

The young man of twenty-four at the "White Horse" in Friday Street is Tom Nash; and it is Peele who is swearing that he is a monstrous clever fellow, and helping him to finish his wine. But Peele is glad to see Ned and Cowley in the doorway, for Tom has a weakness for reading aloud the good things from his own manuscripts. There is only one of the company who is not now sick to death of Nash's satires on Martin Marprelate; and perhaps even he has had enough of them, only he is as yet too obscure a person to say so. That is Will; and Nash detains him for a moment just to listen to his last words on the Marprelate controversy. Marprelate now appears "with a wit worn into the socket, twingling and pinking like the snuffe of a candle; *quantum mutatus ab illo!* how unlike the knave he was before, not for malice but for sharpness. The hogshead was even come to the hauncing, and nothing could be drawne from him but dregs." Will says it is very good; and Nash smiles to himself as he puts the papers in his pockets and thinks vaguely that he might do something for Will. Shakspeare is not a univer-

sity man, and they say he held horses at the doors
of the "Globe" not long ago; but he knows a
good thing when he hears it.

All this time Marlowe is at the "Globe," wondering why the others are so long in coming; but
not wondering very much — for it is good wine
they give you at the "Globe." Even before the
feast is well begun Kit's eyes are bloodshot and
his hands unsteady. Death is already seeking for
him at a tavern in Deptford, and the last scene in
a wild, brief life starts up before us. A miserable
alehouse, drunken words, the flash of a knife, and
a man of genius has received his death-blow.
What an epitaph for the greatest might-have-been
in English literature : "Christopher Marlowe, slain
by a serving-man in a drunken brawl, aged twenty-
nine!" But by the time Shakspeare had reached
his fortieth birthday every one of his fellow-play-
wrights round that table had rushed to his death.

The short stout gentleman who is fond of making jokes, and not particular whom he confides
them to, has heard another good story about Tar-
leton. This is the low comedian Kempe, who
stepped into the shoes of flat-nosed squinting Tar-
leton the other day, but never quite manages to
fill them. He whispers the tale across Will's back
to Cowley, before it is made common property;
and little fancies, as he does so, that any immor-
tality he and his friend may gain will be owing to

their having played, before the end of the sixteenth century, the parts of Dogberry and Verges in a comedy by Shakspeare, whom they are at present rather in the habit of patronizing. The story is received with boisterous laughter, for it suits the time and place.

Peele is in the middle of a love-song when Kit stumbles across the room to say a kind word to Shakspeare. That is a sign that George is not yet so very tipsy; for he is a gallant and a squire of dames so long as he is sober. There is not a maid in any tavern in Fleet Street who does not think George Peele the properest man in London. And yet, Greene being absent, scouring the street with Cutting Ball — whose sister is mother of poor Fortunatus Greene — Peele is the most dissolute man in the "Globe" to-night. There is a sad little daughter sitting up for him at home, and she will have to sit wearily till morning. Marlowe's praises would sink deeper into Will's heart if the author of the "Jew of Malta" were less unsteady on his legs. And yet he takes Kit's words kindly, and is glad to hear that "Titus Andronicus," produced the other day, pleases the man whose praise is most worth having. Will Shakspeare looks up to Kit Marlowe, and "Titus Andronicus" is the work of a young playwright who has tried to write like Kit. Marlowe knows it, and he takes it as something of a compliment,

MY LADY NICOTINE

though he does not believe in imitation himself.
He would return now to his seat beside Ned
Alleyn; but the floor of the room is becoming
unsteady, and Ned seems a long way off. Besides,
Shakspeare's cup would never require refilling if
there were not some one there to help him drink.

The fun becomes fast and furious; and the landlord of the "Globe" puts in an appearance, osten-
sibly to do his guests honour by serving them
himself. But he is fearful of how the rioting may
end, and, if he dared, he would turn Nash into the
street. Tom is the only man there whom the
landlord — if that man had only been a Boswell!
— personally dislikes; indeed Nash is no great
favourite even with his comrades. He has a bitter
tongue, and his heart is not to be mellowed by
wine. The table roars over his sallies, of which
the landlord himself is dimly conscious that he is
the butt, and Kempe and Cowley wince under his
satire. Those excellent comedians fall out over a
trifling difference of opinion; and handsome Nash
— he tells us himself that he was handsome, so
there can be no doubt about it — maintains that
they should decide the dispute by fisticuffs without further loss of time. While Kempe and Cowley threaten to break each other's heads — which,
indeed, would be no great matter if they did it
quietly — Burbage is reciting vehemently, with
no one heeding him; and Marlowe insists on

quarrelling with Armin about the existence of a deity. For when Kit is drunk he is an infidel. Armin will not quarrel with anybody, and Marlowe is exasperated.

But where is Shakspeare all this time? He has retired to a side-table with Alleyn, who has another historical play that requires altering. Their conversation is of comparatively little importance; what we are to note with bated breath is that Will is filling a pipe. His face is placid, for he does not know that the tobacco Ned is handing him is the Arcadia Mixture. I love Ned Alleyn, and like to think that Shakspeare got the Arcadia from him.

For a moment let us turn from Shakspeare at this crisis in his life. Alleyn has left him and is paying the score. Marlowe remains where he fell. Nash has forgotten where he lodges, and so sets off with Peele to an alehouse in Pye Corner where George is only too well known. Kempe and Cowley are sent home in baskets.

Again we turn to the figure in the corner, and there is such a light on his face that we shade our eyes. He is smoking the Arcadia, and as he smokes the tragedy of Hamlet takes form in his brain.

This is the picture that Scrymgeour will never dare to paint. I know that there is no mention of tobacco in Shakspeare's plays, but those who smoke the Arcadia tell their secret to none, and of other mixtures they scorn to speak.

CHAPTER XIV

MY BROTHER HENRY

STRICTLY speaking I never had a brother Henry,
and yet I cannot say that Henry was an impostor.
He came into existence in a curious way, and I
can think of him now without malice as a child of
smoke. The first I heard of Henry was at Pettigrew's house, which is in a London suburb, so con-
veniently situated that I can go there and back in
one day. I was testing some new Cabanas, I remember, when Pettigrew remarked that he had
been lunching with a man who knew my brother
Henry. Not having any brother but Alexander I
felt that Pettigrew had mistaken the name. " Oh
no," Pettigrew said; " he spoke of Alexander too."
Even this did not convince me, and I asked my
host for his friend's name. Scudamour was the
name of the man, and he had met my brothers
Alexander and Henry years before in Paris. Then
I remembered Scudamour, and I probably frowned,
for I myself was my own brother Henry. I distinctly recalled Scudamour meeting Alexander and
me in Paris, and calling me Henry, though my
name begins with J. I explained the mistake to

Pettigrew, and here, for the time being, the matter rested. However, I had by no means heard the last of Henry.

Several times afterwards I heard from various persons that Scudamour wanted to meet me because he knew my brother Henry. At last we did meet, in Jimmy's chambers; and, almost as soon as he saw me, Scudamour asked where Henry was now. This was precisely what I feared. I am a man who always looks like a boy. There are few persons of my age in London who retain their boyish appearance as long as I have done; indeed, this is the curse of my life. Though I am approaching the age of thirty, I pass for twenty; and I have observed old gentlemen frown at my precocity when I said a good thing or helped myself to a second glass of wine. There was, therefore, nothing surprising in Scudamour's remark, that, when he had the pleasure of meeting Henry, Henry must have been about the age that I had now reached. All would have been well had I explained the real state of affairs to this annoying man; but, unfortunately for myself, I loathe entering upon explanations to anybody about anything. This it is to smoke the Arcadia. When I ring for a time-table and William John brings coals instead I accept the coals as a substitute. Much, then, did I dread a discussion with Scudamour, his surprise when he heard that I was

Henry, and his comments on my youthful appearance. Besides, I was smoking the best of all mixtures. There was no likelihood of my meeting Scudamour again, so the easiest way to get rid of him seemed to be to humour him. I therefore told him that Henry was in India, married, and doing well. "Remember me to Henry when you write him," was Scudamour's last remark to me that evening.

A few weeks later some one tapped me on the shoulder in Oxford Street. It was Scudamour. "Heard from Henry?" he asked. I said I had heard by the last mail. "Anything particular in the letter?" I felt that it would not do to say that there was nothing particular in a letter which had come all the way from India, so I hinted that Henry was having trouble with his wife. By this I meant that her health was bad; but he took it up in another way, and I did not set him right. "Ah, ah!" he said, shaking his head sagaciously, "I'm sorry to hear that. Poor Henry!" "Poor old boy!" was all I could think of replying. "How about the children?" Scudamour asked. "Oh, the children," I said, with what I thought presence of mind, "are coming to England." "To stay with Alexander?" he asked. My answer was that Alexander was expecting them by the middle of next month; and eventually Scudamour went away muttering, "Poor Henry!" In a month or so we met again. "No word of Henry's getting leave of absence?" asked Scudamour. I replied shortly that Henry had gone to live in Bombay, and would not be home for years. He saw that I was brusque, so what does he do but draw me aside for a quiet explanation. "I suppose," he said, "you are annoyed because I told Pettigrew that Henry's wife had run away from him. The fact is, I did it for your good. You see I happened to make a remark to Pettigrew about your brother Henry, and he said that there was no such person. Of course I laughed at that, and pointed out not only that I had the pleasure of Henry's acquaintance but that you and I had a talk about the old fellow every time we met. 'Well,' Pettigrew said, 'this is a most remarkable thing; for he,' meaning you, 'said to me in this very room, sitting in that very chair, that Alexander was his only brother.' I saw that Pettigrew resented your concealing the existence of your brother Henry from him, so I thought the most friendly thing I could do was to tell him that your reticence was doubtless due to the unhappy state of poor Henry's private affairs. Naturally in the circumstances you did not want to talk about Henry." I shook Scudamour by the hand, telling him that he had acted judiciously; but if I could have stabbed him in the back at that moment I dare say I would have done it.

I did not see Scudamour again for a long time, for I took care to keep out of his way; but I heard first from him and then of him. One day he wrote to me saying that his nephew was going to Bombay, and would I be so good as to give the youth an introduction to my brother Henry? He also asked me to dine with him and his nephew. I declined the dinner, but I sent the nephew the required note of introduction to Henry. The next I heard of Scudamour was from Pettigrew. "By the way," said Pettigrew, "Scudamour is in Edinburgh at present." I trembled, for Edinburgh is where Alexander lives. "What has taken him there?" I asked, with assumed carelessness. Pettigrew believed it was business; "but," he added, "Scudamour asked me to tell you that he meant to call on Alexander, as he was anxious to see Henry's children." A few days afterwards I had a telegram from Alexander, who generally uses this means of communication when he corresponds with me. "Do you know a man Scudamour? Reply," was what Alexander said. I thought of answering that we had met a man of that name when we were in Paris; but, after consideration, I replied boldly: "Know no one of name of Scudamour."

About two months ago I passed Scudamour in Regent Street, and he scowled at me. This I could have borne if there had been no more of

Henry; but I knew that Scudamour was now telling everybody about Henry's wife. By and by I got a letter from an old friend of Alexander's asking me if there was any truth in a report that Alexander was going to Bombay. Soon afterwards Alexander wrote to me saying he had been told by several persons that I was going to Bombay. In short, I saw that the time had come for killing Henry. So I told Pettigrew that Henry had died of fever, deeply regretted; and asked him to be sure to tell Scudamour, who had always been interested in the deceased's welfare. Pettigrew afterwards told me that he had communicated the sad intelligence to Scudamour. "How did he take it?" I asked. "Well," Pettigrew said, reluctantly, "he told me that when he was up in Edinburgh he did not get on well with Alexander. But he expressed great curiosity as to Henry's children." "Ah," I said, "the children were both drowned in the Forth; a sad affair — we can't bear to talk of it." I am not likely to see much of Scudamour again, nor is Alexander. Scudamour now goes about saying that Henry was the only one of us he really liked.

CHAPTER XV

HOUSE-BOAT "ARCADIA"

SCRYMGEOUR had a house-boat called, of course, the *Arcadia*, to which he was so ill-advised as to invite us all at once. He was at that time lying near Cookham, attempting to catch the advent of summer on a canvas, and we were all, unhappily, able to accept his invitation. Looking back to this nightmare of a holiday, I am puzzled at our not getting on well together, for who should be happy in a house-boat if not five bachelors, well known to each other, and all smokers of the same tobacco? Marriot says now that perhaps we were happy without knowing it; but that is nonsense. We were miserable.

I have concluded that we know each other too well. Though accustomed to gather together in my rooms of an evening in London, we had each his private chambers to retire to, but in the *Arcadia* solitude was impossible. There was no escaping from each other.

Scrymgeour, I think, said that we were unhappy because each of us acted as if the house-boat was his own. We retorted that the boy — by no means a William John — was at the bottom of our troubles, and then Scrymgeour said that he had always been against having a boy. We had been opposed to a boy at first, too, fancying that we should enjoy doing our own cooking. Seeing that there were so many of us this should not have been difficult, but the kitchen was small, and we were always striking against each other and knocking things over. We had to break a window-pane to let the smoke out; then Gilray, in kicking the stove because he had burned his fingers on it, upset the thing, and, before we had time to intervene, a leg of mutton jumped out and darted into the coal-bunk. Jimmy foolishly placed our six tumblers on the window-sill to dry, and a gust of wind toppled them into the river. The draughts were a nuisance. This was owing to windows facing each other being left open, and as a result articles of clothing disappeared so mysteriously that we thought there must be a thief or a somnambulist on board. The third or fourth day, however, going into the saloon unexpectedly, I caught my straw hat disappearing out at the window on the wings of the wind. When last seen it was on its way to Maidenhead, bowling along at the rate of several miles an hour. So we thought it would be as well to have a boy. As far as I remember, this was the only point unanimously agreed upon during the whole time we were aboard. They told us at the Ferry Hotel that boys were rather difficult to get in Cookham; but we instituted a vigorous house-to-house search, and at last we ran a boy to earth and carried him off.

It was most unfortunate for all concerned that the boy did not sleep on board. There was, however, no room for him; so he came at seven in the morning, and retired when his labours were over for the day. I say he came; but in point of fact that was the difficulty with the boy. He couldn't come. He came as far as he could: that is to say, he walked up the tow-path until he was opposite the house-boat, and then he hallooed to be taken on board, whereupon some one had to go in the dingey for him. All the time we were in the house-boat that boy was never five minutes late. Wet or fine, calm or rough, 7 a.m. found the boy on the tow-path hallooing. No sooner were we asleep than the dewy morn was made hideous by the boy. Lying in bed with the blankets over our heads to deaden his cries, his fresh, lusty young voice pierced woodwork, blankets, sheets, everything. "Ya-ho, ahoy, ya ho, aho, ahoy!" So he kept it up. What followed may easily be guessed. We all lay as silent as the grave, each waiting for some one else to rise and bring the impatient lad across. At last the stillness would be broken by some one's yelling out that he would do for that boy. A second would mutter horribly in his

sleep; a third would make himself a favourite for
the moment by shouting through the wooden par-
tition that it was the fifth's turn this morning.
The fifth would tell us where he would see the
boy before he went across for him. Then there
would be silence again. Eventually some one
would put an ulster over his night-shirt, and sternly
announce his intention of going over and taking
the boy's life. Hearing this, the others at once
dropped off to sleep. For a few days we managed
to trick the boy by pulling up our blinds and so
conveying to his mind the impression that we were
getting up. Then he had not our breakfast ready
when we did get up, which naturally enraged us.

As soon as he got on board that boy made his
presence felt. He was very strong and energetic
in the morning, and spent the first half-hour or so
in flinging coals at each other. This was his way
of breaking them; and he was by nature so pa-
tient and humble that he rather flattered himself
when a coal broke at the twentieth attempt. We
used to dream that he was breaking coals on our
heads. Often one of us dashed into the kitchen,
threatening to drop him into the river if he did not
sit quite still on a chair for the next two hours.
Under these threats he looked sufficiently scared
to satisfy anybody; but as soon as all was quiet
again he crept back to the coal-bunk and was at
his old games.

It didn't matter what we did, the boy put a stop to it. We tried whist, and in ten minutes there was a " Hoy, hie, ya-ho!" from the opposite shore. It was the boy come back with the vegetables. If we were reading, " Ya-ho, hie!" and some one had to cross for that boy and the water-can. The boy was on the tow-path just when we had fallen into a snooze; he had to be taken across for the milk immediately we had lit our pipes. On the whole it is an open question whether it was not even more annoying to take him over than to go for him. Two or three times we tried to be sociable and went into the village together; but no sooner had we begun to enjoy ourselves than we remembered that we must go back and let the boy ashore. Tennyson speaks of a company making believe to be merry while all the time the spirit of a departed one haunted them in their play. That was exactly the effect of the boy on us.

Even without the boy I hardly think we should have been a sociable party. The sight of so much humanity gathered in one room became a nuisance. We resorted to all kinds of subterfuge to escape from each other; and the one who finished breakfast first generally managed to make off with the dingey. The others were then at liberty to view him in the distance, in midstream, lying on his back in the bottom of the boat; and it was almost more than we could stand. The only way to bring him back was to bribe the boy into saying that he wanted to go across to the village for bacon or black-lead or sardines. Thus even the boy had his uses.

Things gradually got worse and worse. I remember only one day when as many as four of us were on speaking terms. Even this temporary sociability was only brought about in order that we might combine and fall upon Jimmy, with the more crushing force. Jimmy had put us in an article, representing himself as a kind of superior person who was making a study of us. The thing was such a gross caricature, and so dull, that it was Jimmy we were sorry for rather than ourselves. Still, we gathered round him in a body and told him what we thought of the matter. Affairs might have gone more smoothly after this if we four had been able to hold together. Unfortunately Jimmy won Marriot over, and next day there was a row all round, which resulted in our division into five parties.

One day Pettigrew visited us. He brought his Gladstone bag with him, but did not stay over night. He was glad to go; for at first none of us, I am afraid, was very civil to him, though we afterwards thawed a little. He returned to London and told every one how he found us. I admit we were not prepared to receive company. The house-boat consisted of five apartments — a saloon,

three bedrooms and a kitchen. When he boarded
us we were distributed as follows: I sat smoking
in the saloon, Marriot sat smoking in the first
bedroom, Gilray in the second, Jimmy in the
third, and Scrymgeour in the kitchen. The boy
did not keep Scrymgeour company. He had been
ordered on deck, where he sat with his legs crossed,
the picture of misery because he had no coals to
break. A few days after Pettigrew's visit we followed him to London (leaving Scrymgeour behind), where we soon became friendly again.

CHAPTER XVI

THE ARCADIA MIXTURE AGAIN

ONE day, some weeks after we had left Scrymgeour's house-boat, I was alone in my rooms, very busy smoking, when William John entered with a telegram. It was from Scrymgeour and said, "You have got me into a dreadful mess. Come down here first train."

Wondering what mess I could have got Scrymgeour into I good-naturedly obeyed his summons, and soon I was smoking placidly on the deck of the house-boat, while Scrymgeour, sullen and nervous, tramped back and forward. I saw quickly that the only tobacco had something to do with his troubles, for he began by announcing that one evening soon after we left him he found that he had smoked all his Arcadia. He would have despatched the boy to London for it, but the boy had been all day in the village buying a loaf, and would not be back for hours. Cookham cigars Scrymgeour could not smoke; cigarettes he only endured if made from the Arcadia.

At Cookham he could only get tobacco that

made him uncomfortable. Having recently begun to use a new pouch, he searched his pockets
in vain for odd shreds of the Mixture to which he
had so contemptibly become a slave. In a very
bad temper he took to his dingey, vowing for a
little while that he would violently break the
chains that bound him to one tobacco, and afterwards, when he was restored to his senses, that he
would jilt the Arcadia gradually. He had pulled
some distance down the river, without regarding
the Cliveden Woods, when he all but ran into a
blaze of Chinese lanterns. It was a house-boat
called — let us change its name to the *Heathen
Chinee*. Staying his dingey with a jerk, Scrymgeour
looked up, when a wonderful sight met his eyes.
On the open window of an apparently empty
saloon stood a round tin of tobacco, marked " Arcadia Mixture."

Scrymgeour sat gaping. The only sound to be
heard, except a soft splash of water under the
house-boat, came from the kitchen, where a servant was breaking crockery for supper. The romantic figure in the dingey stretched out his hand
and then drew it back, remembering that there
was a law against this sort of thing. He thought
to himself, " If I were to wait until the owner returns, no doubt a man who smokes the Arcadia
would feel for me." Then his fatal horror of explanations whispered to him, " The owner may be

a stupid, garrulous fellow who will detain you here half the night explaining your situation." Scrymgeour, I want to impress upon the reader, was, like myself, the sort of man who, if asked whether he did not think "In Memoriam" Mr. Browning's greatest poem, would say Yes, as the easiest way of ending the conversation. Obviously he would save himself trouble by simply annexing the tin. He seized it and rowed off.

Smokers, who know how tobacco develops the finer feelings, hardly require to be told what happened next. Suddenly Scrymgeour remembered that he was probably leaving the owner of the *Heathen Chinee* without any Arcadia Mixture. He at once filled his pouch, and, pulling softly back to the house-boat, replaced the tin on the window, his bosom swelling with the pride of those who give presents. At the same moment a hand gripped him by the neck, and a girl, somewhere on deck, screamed.

Scrymgeour's captor, who was no other than the owner of the *Heathen Chinee*, dragged him fiercely into the house-boat and stormed at him for five minutes. My friend shuddered as he thought of the explanations to come when he was allowed to speak, and gradually he realized that he had been mistaken for some one else — apparently for some young blade who had been carrying on a clandestine flirtation with the old gentleman's daughter.

It will take an hour, thought Scrymgeour, to convince him that I am not that person, and another hour to explain why I am really here. Then the weak creature had an idea : " Might not the simplest plan be to say that his surmises are correct, promise to give his daughter up, and row away as quickly as possible ? " He began to wonder if the girl was pretty; but he saw it would hardly do to say that he reserved his defence until he could see her.

" I admit," he said, at last, " that I admire your daughter; but she spurned my advances, and we parted yesterday forever."

" Yesterday ! "

" Or was it the day before ? "

" Why, sir, I have caught you red-handed ! "

" This is an accident," Scrymgeour explained, " and I promise never to speak to her again." Then he added as an after-thought, " however painful that may be to me."

Before Scrymgeour returned to his dingey he had been told that he would be drowned if he came near that house-boat again. As he sculled away he had a glimpse of the flirting daughter, whom he described to me briefly as being of such engaging appearance that six yards was a trying distance to be away from her.

" Here," thought Scrymgeour that night over a pipe of the Mixture, " the affair ends; though I dare say the young lady will call me terrible names when she hears that I have personated her lover. I must take care to avoid the father now, for he will feel that I have been fooling him. Perhaps I should have made a clean breast of it ; but I do loathe explanations."

Two days afterwards Scrymgeour passed the father and daughter on the river. The lady said " Thank you " to him with her eyes, and, still more remarkable, the old gentleman bowed. Scrymgeour thought it over. " She is grateful to me," he concluded, " for drawing away suspicion from the other man, but what can have made the father so amiable ? Suppose she has not told him that I am an impostor, he should still look upon me as a villain ; and if she has told him, he should be still more furious. It is curious, but no affair of mine." Three times within the next few days he encountered the lady on the tow-path or elsewhere with a young gentleman of empty countenance, who, he saw, must be the real Lothario. Once they passed him when he was in the shadow of a tree, and the lady was making pretty faces with a cigarette in her mouth. The house-boat *Heathen Chinee* lay but a short distance off; and Scrymgeour could see the owner gazing after his daughter placidly, a pipe between his lips. " He must be approving of her conduct now," was my friend's natural conclusion. Then one forenoon Scrym-

geour travelled to town in the same compartment
as the old gentleman, who was exceedingly frank,
and made sly remarks about romantic young people who met by stealth when there was no reason
why they should not meet openly. " What does
he mean?" Scrymgeour asked himself uneasily.
He saw terribly elaborate explanations gathering,
and shrank from them.

Then Scrymgeour was one day out in a punt,
when he encountered the old gentleman in a canoe.
The old man said, purple with passion, that he
was on his way to pay Mr. Scrymgeour a business
visit. " Oh, yes," he continued, " I know who
you are; if I had not discovered you were a man
of means I would not have let the thing go on,
and now I insist on an explanation."

Explanations!

They made for Scrymgeour's house-boat, with
almost no words on the young man's part; but the
father blurted out several things — as that his
daughter knew where he was going when he left
the *Heathen Chinee*, and that he had an hour before
seen Scrymgeour making love to another girl.

" Don't deny it!" cried the indignant father; " I
recognized you by your velvet coat and broad
hat."

Then Scrymgeour began to see more clearly.
The girl had encouraged the deception, and had
been allowed to meet her lover because he was

supposed to be no adventurer but the wealthy Mr. Scrymgeour. She must have told the fellow to get a coat and hat like his to help the plot. At the time the artist only saw all this in a jumble.

Scrymgeour had bravely resolved to explain everything now; but his bewilderment may be conceived when, on entering his saloon with the lady's father, the first thing they saw was the lady herself. The old gentleman gasped, and his daughter looked at Scrymgeour imploringly.

" Now," said the father, fiercely, " explain!"

The lady's tears became her vastly. Hardly knowing what he did, Scrymgeour put his arm round her.

" Well, go on," I said, when at this point Scrymgeour stopped.

" There is no more to tell," he replied; " you see the girl allowed me to — well, protect her — and — and the old gentleman thinks we are engaged."

" I don't wonder. What does the lady say?"

" She says that she ran along the bank and got into my house-boat by the plank, meaning to see me before her father arrived and to entreat me to run away."

" With her?"

" No, without her."

" But what does she say about explaining matters to her father?"

" She says she dare not, and as for me, I could not. That was why I telegraphed to you."

" You want me to be intercessor ? No, Scrymgeour; your only honourable course is marriage."

" But you must help me. It is all your fault, teaching me to like the Arcadia Mixture."

I thought this so impudent of Scrymgeour that I bade him good-night at once. All the men on the stair are still confident that he would have married her had the lady not cut the knot by eloping with Scrymgeour's double.

CHAPTER XVII

THE ROMANCE OF A PIPE-CLEANER

WE continued to visit the *Arcadia*, though only one at a time now, and Gilray who went most frequently also remained longest. In other words he was in love again, and this time she lived at Cookham. Marriot's love affairs I pushed from me with a wave of my pipe, but Gilray's second case was serious.

In time, however, he returned to the Arcadia Mixture, though not until the house-boat was in its winter quarters. I witnessed his complete recovery, the scene being his chambers. Really it is rather a pathetic story, and so I give the telling of it to a rose, which the lady once presented to Gilray. Conceive the rose lying, as I saw it, on Gilray's hearthrug, and then imagine it whispering as follows:

"A wire was round me that white night on the river when she let him take me from her. Then I hated the wire. Alas! hear the end.

"My moments are numbered; and if I would expose him with my dying sigh, I must not sentimentalize over my own decay. They were in a punt, her hand trailing in the water, when I became his. When they parted that night at Cookham Lock he held her head in his hands, and they gazed into each other's eyes. Then he turned away quickly; when he reached the punt again he was whistling. Several times before we came to the house-boat in which he and another man lived, he felt in his pocket to make sure that I was still there. At the house-boat he put me in a tumbler of water out of sight of his friend, and frequently he stole to the spot like a thief to look at me. Early next morning he put me in his button-hole, calling me sweet names. When his friend saw me he too whistled, but not in the same way. Then my owner glared at him. This happened many months ago.

" Next evening I was in a garden that slopes to the river. I was on his breast, and so for a moment was she. His voice was so soft and low as he said to her the words he had said to me the night before, that I slumbered in a dream. When I awoke suddenly he was raging at her, and she cried. I know not why they quarrelled so quickly, but it was about some one whom he called ' that fellow,' while she called him ' a friend of papa's.' He looked at her for a long time again, and then said coldly that he wished her a very good-evening. She bowed and went toward a house, humming a merry air, while he pretended to light a cigarette made from a tobacco of which he was very fond. Till very late that night I heard him walking up and down the deck of the house-boat, his friend shouting to him not to be an ass. Me he had flung fiercely on the floor of the house-boat. About midnight he came downstairs, his face white, and, snatching me up, put me in his pocket· Again we went into the punt, and he pushed it within sight of the garden. There he pulled in his pole and lay groaning in the punt, letting it drift, while he called her his beloved and a little devil. Suddenly he took me from his pocket, kissed me and cast me from him into the night. I fell among reeds, head downwards; and there I lay all through the cold, horrid night. The gray morning came at last, then the sun, and a boat now and again. I thought I had found my grave, when I saw his punt coming towards the reeds. He searched everywhere for me, and at last he found me. So delighted and affectionate was he that I forgave him my sufferings; only I was jealous of a letter in his other pocket, which he read over many times, murmuring that it explained everything.

"Her I never saw again, but I heard her voice. He kept me now in a leather case in an inner pocket, where I was squeezed very flat. What they said to each other I could not catch; but I understood afterwards, for he always repeated to me what he had been saying to her, and many times he was loving, many times angry, like a bad man. At last came a day when he had a letter from her containing many things he had given her, among them a ring on which she had seemed to set great store. What it all meant I never rightly knew, but he flung the ring into the Thames, calling her all the old wicked names and some new ones. I remember how we rushed to her house, along the bank this time, and that she asked him to be her brother; but he screamed denunciations at her, again speaking of 'that fellow,' and saying that he was going to-morrow to Manitoba.

"So far as I know they saw each other no more. He walked on the deck so much now that his friend went back to London, saying he could get no sleep. Sometimes we took long walks alone; often we sat for hours looking at the river, for on those occasions he would take me out of the leather case and put me on his knee. One day his friend came back and told him that he would soon get over it, he himself having once had a similar experience; but my master said no one had ever loved as he had loved, and muttered 'Vixi, vixi' to himself till the other told him not to be a fool, but to come to the hotel and have something to eat. Over this they quarrelled, my master hinting that he would eat no more; but he ate heartily after his friend was gone.

"After a time we left the house-boat, and were in chambers in a great Inn. I was still in his pocket, and heard many conversations between him and people who came to see him, and he would tell them that he loathed the society of women. When they told him, as one or two did, that they were in love, he always said that he had gone through that stage ages ago. Still, at nights he would take me out of my case, when he was alone, and look at me; after which he walked up and down the room in an agitated manner, and cried, 'Vixi.'

" By and by he left me in a coat that he was no longer wearing. Before this he had always put me into whatever coat he had on. I lay neglected, I think, for a month, until one day he felt the pockets of the coat for something else, and pulled me out. I don't think he remembered what was in the leather case at first; but as he looked at me his face filled with sentiment, and next day he took me with him to Cookham. The winter was come, and it was a cold day. There were no boats on the river. He walked up the bank to the garden where was the house in which she had lived; but the place was now deserted. On the garden-gate he sat down, taking me from his pocket; and here, I think, he meant to recall the days that were dead.   But a cold, piercing wind was blowing, and many times he looked at his watch, putting it to his ear as if he thought it had stopped.   After a little he took to flinging stones into the water, for something to do; and then he went to the hotel and stayed there till he got a train back to London.   We were home many hours before he meant to be back, and that night he went to a theatre.

" That was my last day in the leather case. He keeps something else in it now.   He flung me among old papers, smoking-caps, slippers, and other odds-and-ends into a box, where I have remained until to-night.   A month or more ago he rummaged in the box for some old letters, and coming upon me unexpectedly he jagged his finger on the wire. ' Where on earth did you come from ? ' he asked me.   Then he remembered, and flung me back among the papers with a laugh. Now we come to to-night.   An hour ago I heard him blowing down something, then stamping his feet.   From his words I knew that his pipe was stopped.   I heard him ring a bell and ask angrily who had gone off with his pipe-cleaners.   He bustled through the room looking for them or for a substitute, and after a time he cried aloud, ' I have it ; that would do ; but where was it I saw the thing last ? '   He pulled out several drawers, looked through his desk, and then opened the box in which

I lay.   He tumbled its contents over until he found me, and then he pulled me out, exclaiming, 'Eureka!'   My heart sank, for I understood all as I fell leaf by leaf on the hearthrug where I now lie. He took the wire off me and used it to clean his pipe."

CHAPTER XVIII

WHAT COULD HE DO?

THIS was another of Marriot's perplexities of the heart. He had been on the Continent, and I knew from his face, the moment he returned, that I would have a night of him.

"On the 4th of September," he began, playing agitatedly with my tobacco-pouch, which was not for hands like his, "I had walked from Spondinig to Franzenshöhe, which is a Tyrolese inn near the top of the Stelvio Pass. From the inn to a very fine glacier is only a stroll of a few minutes; but the path is broken by a roaring stream. The only bridge across this stream is a plank, which seemed to give way as I put my foot on it. I drew back, for the stream would be called one long waterfall in England. Though a passionate admirer of courage, I easily lose my head myself, and I did not dare to venture across the plank. I walked up the stream, looking in vain for another crossing; and finally sat down on a wilderness of stones, from which I happened to have a good view of the plank. In parties of two and three a number of tourists strolled down the path; but they were all afraid to cross the bridge. I saw them test it with their alpenstocks; but none would put more than one foot on it. They gathered there at their wits' end. Suddenly I saw that there was some one on the plank. It was a young lady. I stood up and gazed. She was perhaps a hundred yards away from me; but I could distinctly make out her swaying, girlish figure, her deerstalker cap, and the ends of her boa (as, I think, those long furry things are called) floating in the wind. In a moment she was safe on the other side; but on the middle of the plank she had turned to kiss her hand to some of her more timid friends, and it was then that I fell in love with her. No doubt it was the very place for romance, if one was sufficiently clad; but I am not 'susceptible,' as it is called, and I had never loved before. On the other hand, I was always a firm believer in love at first sight, which, as you will see immediately, is at the very root of my present sufferings.

"The other tourists, their fears allayed, now crossed the plank, but I hurried away anywhere; and found myself an hour afterwards on a hillside, surrounded by tinkling cows. All that time I had been thinking of a plank with a girl on it. I returned hastily to the inn, to hear that the heroine of the bridge and her friends had already driven off up the pass. My intention had been to stay at Franzenshöhe over night, but of course I at once followed the line of carriages which could be seen crawling up the winding road. It was no difficult matter to overtake them, and in half an hour I was within a few yards of the hindmost carriage. It contained her of whom I was in pursuit. Her back was toward me, but I recognized the cap and the boa. I confess that I was nervous about her face, which I had not yet seen. So often had I been disappointed in ladies when they showed their faces, that I muttered Jimmy's aphorism to myself: 'The saddest thing in life is that most women look best from the back.' But when she looked round all anxiety was dispelled. So far as your advice is concerned, it cannot matter to you what she was like. Briefly she was charming.

" I am naturally shy, and so had more difficulty in making her acquaintance than many travellers would have had. It was at the Baths of Bormio that we came together. I had bribed a waiter to seat me next her father at dinner; but, when the time came, I could say nothing to him, so anxious was I to create a favourable impression. In the evening, however, I found the family gathered round a pole, with skittles at the foot of it. They were wondering how Italian skittles was played, and, though I had no idea, I volunteered to teach them. Fortunately, none of them understood Italian, and consequently the expostulations of the boy in charge were disregarded. It is not my intention to dwell upon the never-to-be-forgotten days — ah, and still more the evenings! — we spent at the Baths of Bormio. I had loved her as she crossed the plank; but daily now had I more cause to love her, and it was at Bormio that she learned — I say it with all humility — to love me. The seat in the garden on which I proposed is doubtless still to be seen, with the chair near it on which her papa was at that very moment sitting, with one of his feet on a small table. During the three sunny days that followed, my life was one delicious dream, with no sign that the awakening was at hand.

"So far I had not mentioned the incident at Franzenshöhe to her. Perhaps you will call my reticence contemptible; but the fact is, I feared to fall in her esteem. I could not have spoken of the plank without admitting that I was afraid to cross it; and then what would she, who was a heroine, think of a man who was so little of a hero? Thus, though I had told her many times that I fell in love with her at first sight, she thought I referred to the time when she first saw me. She liked to hear me say that I believed in no love but love at first sight; and, looking back, I can recall saying it at least once on every seat in the garden at the Baths of Bormio.

"Do you know Tirano, a hamlet in a nest of

vines, where Italian soldiers strut and women sleep in the sun beside baskets of fruit? How happily we entered it; were we the same persons who left it within an hour? I was now travelling with her party; and at Tirano, while the others rested, she and I walked down a road between vines and Indian corn. Why I should then have told her that I loved her for a whole day before she saw me I cannot tell. It may have been something she said, perhaps only an irresistible movement of her head; for her grace was ever taking me by surprise, and she was a revelation a thousand times a day. But whatever it was that made me speak out, I suddenly told her that I fell in love with her as she stood upon the plank at Franzenshöhe. I remember her stopping short at a point where there had probably once been a gate to the vineyard, and I thought she was angry with me for not having told her of the Franzens-höhe incident before. Soon the pallor of her face alarmed me. She entreated me to say it was not at Franzenshöhe that I first loved her, and I fancied she was afraid lest her behaviour on the bridge had seemed a little bold. I told her it was divine, and pictured the scene as only an anxious lover could do. Then she burst into tears, and we went back silently to her relatives. She would not say a word to me.

"We drove to Sondrio, and before we reached

it I dare say I was as pale as she. A horrible thought had flashed upon me. At Sondrio I took her papa aside, and, without telling him what had happened, questioned him about his impressions of Franzenshöhe. 'You remember the little bridge,' he said, 'that we were all afraid to cross; by Jove, I have often wondered who that girl was that ventured over it first.'

"I hastened away from him to think. My fears had been confirmed. It was not she who had first crossed the plank. Therefore it was not she with whom I had fallen in love. Nothing could be plainer than that I was in love with the wrong person. All the time I had loved another. But who was she? Besides, did I love her? Certainly not. Yes, but why did I love this one? The whole foundation of my love had been swept away. Yet the love remained. Which is absurd.

"At Colico I put the difficulty to her father; but he is stout, and did not understand its magnitude. He said he could not see how it mattered. As for her, I have never mentioned it to her again; but she is always thinking of it, and so am I. A wall has risen up between us, and how to get over it, or whether I have any right to get over it, I know not. Will you help me — and her?"

"Certainly not," I said.

CHAPTER XIX

PRIMUS

PRIMUS is my brother's eldest son, and he once spent his Easter holidays with me. I did not want him, nor was he anxious to come, but circumstances were too strong for us, and, to be just to Primus, he did his best to show me that I was not in his way. He was then at the age when boys begin to address each other by their surnames.

I have said that I always took care not to know how much tobacco I smoked in a week, and therefore I may be hinting a libel on Primus when I say that while he was with me the Arcadia disappeared mysteriously. Though he spoke respectfully of the Mixture — as became my nephew — he tumbled it on to the table so that he might make a telephone out of the tins, and he had a passion for what he called "snipping cigars." Scrymgeour gave him a cigar-cutter which was pistol-shaped. You put the cigar end on a hole, pulled the trigger, and the cigar was snipped. The simplicity of the thing fascinated Primus, and

128

after his return to school I found that he had broken into my Cabana boxes, and snipped nearly three hundred cigars.

As soon as he arrived Primus laid siege to the heart of William John, captured it in six hours and demoralized it in twenty-four. We who had known William John for years considered him very practical, but Primus fired him with tales of dark deeds at "old Poppy's" — which was Primus's handy name for his preceptor — and in a short time William John was so full of romance that we could not trust him to black our boots. He and Primus had a scheme for seizing a lugger and becoming pirates, when Primus was to be captain, William John first-lieutenant, and old Poppy a prisoner. To the crew was added a boy with a catapult, one Johnny Fox, who was another victim of the tyrant Poppy, and they practiced walking the plank at Scrymgeour's window. The plank was pushed nearly half way out at the window, and you walked up it until it toppled and you were flung into the quadrangle. Such was the romance of William John that he walked the plank with his arms tied, shouting scornfully, by request, " Captain Kydd, I defy you, ha, ha, the buccaneer does not live who will blanch the cheeks of Dick, the Doughty Tar!" Then William John disappeared, and had to be put in poultices.

While William John was in bed slowly recov-

ering from his heroism, the pirate captain and
Johnny Fox got me into trouble by stretching a
string across the square six feet from the ground,
against which many tall hats struck, to topple in
the dust. An improved sling from the Lowther
Arcade kept the glazier constantly in the Inn.
Primus and Johnny Fox strolled into Holborn,
knocked a bootblack's cap off, and returned with
lumps on their foreheads. They were observed
one day in Hyde Park — whither it may be feared
they had gone with cigarettes — running after
sheep, from which ladies were flying, while street
arabs chased the pirates and a policeman chased
the street arabs. The only book they read was
the " Comic History of Rome," the property of
Gilray. This they liked so much that Primus papered the inside of his box with pictures from it.
The only authors they consulted me about were
"two big swells" called Descartes and James
Payn, of whom Primus discovered that the one
could always work best in bed, while the other
thought Latin and Greek a mistake. It was the
intention of the pirates to call old Poppy's attention to these gentlemen's views.

Soon after Primus came to me I learned that
his schoolmaster had given him a holiday task.
All the " fellows " in his form had to write an essay entitled " My Holidays, and How I Turned
Them to Account," and to send it to their precep-

tor. Primus troubled his head little about the task while the composition of it was yet afar off; but as his time drew near he referred to it with indignation and to his master's action in prescribing it as a "low trick." He frightened the housekeeper into tears by saying that he would not write a line of the task, and, what was more, he would "cheek" his master for imposing it; and I also heard that he and Johnny had some thought of writing the essay in a form suggested by their perusal of the "Comic History of Rome." One day I found a paper in my chambers which told me that the task was nevertheless receiving serious consideration. It was the instructions given by Primus's master with regard to the essay, which was to be "in the form of a letter," and "not less than five hundred words in length." The writer, it was suggested, should give a general sketch of how he was passing his time, what books he was reading, and "how he was making the home brighter." I did not know that Primus had risen equal to the occasion until one day after his departure, when I received his epistle from the schoolmaster, who wanted me to say whether it was a true statement. Here is Primus's essay on his holidays and how he made the home brighter : —

"RESPECTED SIR,— I venture to address you on a subject of jeneral interest to all engaged in edu-

cation, and the subject I venture to address you on
is, 'My Holidays and How I Turned Them to
Account.' Three weeks and two days has now
elapsed since I quited your scholastic establishment, and I quited your scholastic establishment
with tears in my eyes, it being the one of all the
scholastic establishments I have been at that I
loved to reside in, and everybody was of an amiable disposition. Hollidays is good for making us
renew our studdies with redoubled vigour, the
mussels needing to be invigorated, and I have not
overworked mind and body in my hollidays. I
found my uncle well, and drove in a handsome to
the door, and he thought I was much improved
both in apearance and manners; and I said it was
jew to the loving care of my teacher making improvement in apearance and manners a pleasure
to the youth of England. My uncle was partik-
larly pleased with the improvement I had made,
not only in my appearance and manners, but also
in my studdies; and I told him Casear was the
Latin writer I liked best, and quoted ' Veni, vidi,
vici,' and some others which I regret I cannot
mind at present. With your kind permission I
should like to write you a line about how I spend
my days during the hollidays; and my first way of
spending my days during the hollidays is whatsoever
my hands find to do doing it with all my might;
also setting my face nobly against hurting the feal-

ings of others, and minding to say, before I go to sleep, 'Something attempted, something done, to earn a night's repose,' as advised by you, my esteemed communicant. I spend my days during the hollidays getting up early, so as to be down in time for breakfast and not to give no trouble. At breakfast I behave like a model, so as to set a good example; and then I go out a walk with my esteemed young friend John Fox, whom I chose carefully for a friend, fearing to corrupt my morrals by holding communications with rude boys. The J. Fox whom I mention is esteemed by all who knows him as of a unusually gentle disposition; and you know him, respected sir, yourself, he being in my form, and best known in regretble slang as 'Foxy.' We walks in Hyde Park admiring the works of nature, and keeps up our classics when we see a tree by calling it 'arbor' and then going through the declensions; but we never climbs trees for fear of messing the clothes bestowed upon us by our beloved parents in the sweat of their brow; and we scorns to fling stones at the beautiful warblers which fill the atmosfere with music. In the afternoons I spend my days during the hollidays talking with the housekeeper about the things she understands, like not taking off my flannels till June 15, and also praising the matron at the school for seeing about the socks. In the evening I devote myself to whatever good cause I can think of; and I always take off my boots and put on my slippers so as not to soil the carpet. I should like, respected sir, to inform you of the books I read when my duties does not call me elsewhere; and the books I read are the works of William Shakspeare, John Milton, Albert Tennyson, and Francis Bacon. Me and John Fox also reads the ' History of Rome,' so as to prime ourselves with the greatness of the past; and we hopes the glorious examples of Romulus and Remus, but especially Hannibal, will sink into our minds to spur us along. I am desirous to acquaint you with the way I make my uncle's home brighter; but the 500 words is up. So looking forward egerly to resume my studdies, I am, respected sir, your dilligent pupil."

CHAPTER XX

PRIMUS TO HIS UNCLE

THOUGH we all pretended to be glad when Primus went, we spoke of him briefly at times, and I read his letters aloud at our evening meetings. Here is a series of them from my desk. Primus was now a year and a half older, and his spelling had improved.

I

November 16th.

DEAR UNCLE,— Though I have not written to you for a long time I often think about you and Mr. Gilray and the rest and the Arcadia Mixture, and I beg to state that my mother will have informed you I am well and happy but a little overworked, as I am desirous of pleasing my preceptor by obtaining a credible position in the exams and we breakfast at 7.30 sharp. I suppose you are to give me a six-shilling thing again as a Christmas present, so I drop you a line not to buy something I don't want, as it is only thirty-nine days to Christmas. I think I 'll have a book again but not a fairy tale or any of that sort, nor the "Swiss Family Robinson," nor any of the old books. There is a rattling story called "Kidnapped," by H. Rider Haggard, but it is only five shillings, so if you thought of it you could make up the six shillings by giving me a football belt. Last year you gave me "The Formation of Character," and I read it with great mental improvement and all that, but this time I want a change, namely, (1) not a fairy tale, (2) not an old book, (3) not mental improvement book. Don't fix on anything without telling me first what it is. Tell William John I walked into Darky and settled him in three rounds. Best regards to Mr. Gilray and the others.

II

November 19th.

DEAR UNCLE,— Our preceptor is against us writing letters he doesn't see, so I have to carry the paper to the dormitory up my waistcoat and write there, and I wish old Poppy smoked the Arcadia Mixture to make him more like you. Never mind about the football belt, as I got Johnny Fox's for two white mice; so I don't want "Kidnapped," which I wrote about to you, as I want you to stick to six-shilling book. There is one called "Dead Man's Rock" that Dickson Secundus has heard about, and it sounds well; but it is never safe to go by the name, so don't buy it

136

till I hear more about it. If you see biographies of it in the newspapers you might send them to me, as it should be about pirates by the title, but the author does not give his name, which is rather suspicious. So, remember, don't buy it yet, and also find out price, whether illustrated, and how many pages. Ballantyne's story this year is about the fire-brigade; but I don't think I'll have it as he is getting rather informative, and I have one of his about the fire-brigade already. Of course I don't fix not to have it, only don't buy it at present. Don't buy " Dead Man's Rock " either. I am working diligently, and tell the housekeeper my socks is all right. We may fix on " Dead Man's Rock," but it is best not to be in a hurry.

III

November 24th.

DEAR UNCLE,— I don't think I'll have " Dead Man's Rock," as Hope has two stories out this year, and he is a safe man to go to. The worst of it is that they are three-and-six each, and Dickson Secundus says they are continuations of each other, so it is best to have them both or neither. The two at three-and-six would make 7s., and I wonder if you would care to go that length this year. I am getting on first-rate with my Greek, and will do capital if my health does not break down with over-pressure. Perhaps if you bought the two you would get them for 6s. 6d. Or what do you say to the housekeeper's giving a shilling of it, and not sending the neckties?

IV

November 26th.

DEAR UNCLE,— I was disappointed at not hearing from you this morning, but conclude you are very busy. I don't want Hope's books, but I think I'll rather have a football. We played Gloucester on Tuesday and beat them all to sticks (five goals two tries to one try!!!) It would cost 7s. 6d., and I'll make up the one-and-six myself out of my pocket-money; but you can pay it all just now, and then I'll pay you later when am more flush than I am at present. I'd better buy it myself or you might not get the right kind, so you might send the money in a postal order by return. You get the postal orders at the nearest post-office, and enclose them in a letter. I want the football at once. (1) Not a book of any kind whatever; (2) a football, but I'll buy it myself; (3) price 7s. 6d.; (4) send postal order.

V

November 29th.

DEAR UNCLE,—Kindly inform William John that I am in receipt of his favour of yesterday prox., and also your message, saying am I sure it is a football I want. I have to inform you that I have changed my mind and think I'll stick to a book (or two books according to price) after all. Dickson Secundus has seen a newspaper biography of " Dead Man's Rock " and it is ripping, but unfortunately there is a lot in it about a girl. So don't buy " Dead Man's Rock " for me. I told Fox about Hope's two books and he advises me to get one of them (3s. 6d.), and to take the rest of the money (2s. 6d.) in cash, making in all six shillings. I don't know if I should like that plan, though fair to both parties, as Dickson Secundus once took money from his father instead of a book and it went like winking with nothing left to show for it; but I'll think it over between my scholastic tasks and write to you again, so do nothing till you hear from me, and mind I don't want football.

VI

December 3rd.

DEAR UNCLE,— Don't buy Hope's books. There is a grand story out by Jules Verne, about a man who made a machine that enabled him to walk on his head through space with seventy-five illustrations; but the worst of it is it costs half a guinea. Of course I don't ask you to give so much as that; but it is a pity it costs so much, as it is evidently a ripping book, and nothing like it. Ten-and-six is a lot of money. What do you think ? I enclose for your consideration a newspaper account of it, which says it will fire the imagination and teach boys to be manly and self-reliant. Of course you could not give it to me; but I think it would do me good, and am working so hard that I have no time for physical exercise. It is to be got at all booksellers. P.S.—Fox has read "Dead Man's Rock" and likes it A1.

VII

December 4th.

DEAR UNCLE,— I was thinking about Jules Verne's book last night after I went to bed, and I see a way of getting it which both Dickson Secundus and Fox consider fair. I want you to give it to me as my Christmas present for both this year and next year. Thus I won't want a present from you next Christmas; but I don't mind that so long as I get this book. One six-shilling book this year and another next year would come to 12s., and Jules Verne's book is only 10s. 6d., so this plan will save you 1s. 6d. in the long run. I think you should buy it at once, in case they are all sold out before Christmas.

VIII

December 5th.

MY DEAR UNCLE,— I hope you hav'n't bought the book yet, as Dickson Secundus has found out that there is a shop in the Strand where all the books are sold cheap. You get threepence off every shilling, so you would get a ten-and-six

140

book for 7s. 10½d. That will let you get me a cheapish one next year after all. I enclose the address.

IX

December 7th.

Dear Uncle,—Dickson Secundus was looking to-day at "The Formation of Character," which you gave me last year, and he has found out that it was bought in the shop in the Strand that I wrote you about, so you got it for 4s. 6d. We have been looking up the books I got from you at other Christmases, and they all have the stamp on them which shows they were bought at that shop. Some of them I got when I was a kid, and that was the time you gave me 2s. and 3s. 6d. books; but Dickson Secundus and Fox have been helping me to count up how much you owe me as follows:—

	Nominal price. £ s. d.	Price paid. s. d.
1880 "Sunshine and Shadow"	0 2 0	1 6
1881 "Honesty Jack"	0 2 0	1 6
1882 "The Boy Makes the Man"	0 3 6	2 7½
1883 "Great Explorers"	0 3 6	2 7½
1884 "Shooting the Rapids"	0 3 6	2 7½
1885 "The Boy Voyagers"	0 5 0	3 9
1886 "The Formation of Character"	0 6 0	4 6
	1 5 6	19 1½
	0 19 1½	
	0 6 4½	

141

Thus 6s. 4½d. is the exact sum. The best plan will be for you not to buy anything for me till I get my holidays when my father is to bring me to London. Tell William John I am coming.

P.S.—I told my father about the Arcadia Mixture, and that is why he is coming to London.

CHAPTER XXI

ENGLISH-GROWN TOBACCO

PETTIGREW asked me to come to his house one
evening and test some tobacco that had been
grown in his brother's Devonshire garden. I had
so far had no opportunity of judging for myself
whether this attempt to grow tobacco on English
soil was to succeed. Very complimentary was Pettigrew's assertion that he had restrained himself
from trying the tobacco until we could test it in
company.

At the dinner-table while Mrs. Pettigrew was
present we managed to talk for a time of other
matters; but the tobacco was on our minds, and I
was glad to see that, despite her raillery, my hostess had a genuine interest in the coming experiment. She drew an amusing picture, no doubt
a little exaggerated, of her husband's difficulty in
refraining from testing the tobacco until my arrival, declaring that every time she entered the
smoking-room she found him staring at it. Pettigrew took this in good part, and informed me that
she had carried the tobacco several times into the

143

drawing-room to show it proudly to her friends. He was very delighted, he said, that I was to remain over-night, as that would give us a long evening to test the tobacco thoroughly. A neighbour of his had also been experimenting; and Pettigrew, who has a considerable sense of humour, told me a diverting story about this gentleman and his friends having passed judgment on home-grown tobacco after smoking one pipe of it! We were laughing over the ridiculously unsatisfactory character of this test (so called) when we adjourned to the smoking-room. Before we did so Mrs. Pettigrew bade me good-night. She had also left strict orders with the servants that we were on no account to be disturbed.

As soon as we were comfortably seated in our smoking-chairs, which takes longer than some people think, Pettigrew offered me a Cabana. I would have preferred to begin at once with the tobacco; but of course he was my host, and I put myself entirely in his hands. I noticed that, from the moment his wife left us, he was a little excited, talking more than is his wont. He seemed to think that he was not doing his duty as a host if the conversation flagged for a moment, and what was still more curious, he spoke of everything except his garden-tobacco. I emphasize this here at starting, lest any one should think that I was in any way responsible for the manner in which our experiment was conducted. If fault there was, it lies at Petti-grew's door. I remember distinctly asking him — not in a half-hearted way but boldly — to produce his tobacco. I did this at an early hour of the proceedings, immediately after I had lit a second cigar. The reason I took that cigar will be ob-vious to every gentleman who smokes. Had I declined it, Pettigrew might have thought that I disliked the brand, which would have been pain-ful to him. However, he did not at once bring out the tobacco; indeed, his precise words, I re-member, were that we had lots of time. As his guest I could not press him further.

Pettigrew smokes more quickly than I do, and he had reached the end of his second cigar when there was still five minutes of mine left. It dis-tresses me to have to say what followed. He hastily lit a third cigar, and then, unlocking a cup-board, produced about two ounces of his garden-tobacco. His object was only too plain. Hav-ing just begun a third cigar he could not be expected to try the tobacco at present, but there was nothing to prevent my trying it. I regarded Pettigrew rather contemptuously, and then I looked with much interest at the tobacco. It was of an inky colour. When I looked up I caught Pettigrew's eye on me. He withdrew it hurriedly; but soon afterwards I saw him look-ing in the same sly way again. There was a rather painful silence for a time, and then he asked me if I had anything to say. I replied firmly that I was looking forward to trying the tobacco with very great interest. By this time my cigar was reduced to a stump; but, for reasons that Pettigrew misunderstood, I continued to smoke it. Somehow, our chairs had got out of position now, and we were sitting with our backs to each other. I felt that Pettigrew was looking at me covertly over his shoulder, and took a side-glance to make sure of this. Our eyes met, and I bit my lips. If there is one thing I loathe, it is to be looked at in this shame-faced manner.

I continued to smoke the stump of my cigar until it scorched my under-lip, and at intervals Pettigrew said, without looking round, that my cigar seemed everlasting. I treated his innuendo with contempt; but at last I had to let the cigar-end go. Not to make a fuss I dropped it very quietly; but Pettigrew must have been listening for the sound. He wheeled round at once, and pushed the garden-tobacco toward me. Never, perhaps, have I thought so little of him as at that moment. My indignation probably showed in my face, for he drew back, saying that he thought I "wanted to try it." Now I had never said that I did not want to try it. The reader has seen that I went to Pettigrew's house solely with the object of trying the tobacco. Had Pettigrew, then, any ground for insinuating that I did not mean to try it? Restraining my passion I lit a third cigar, and then put the question to him bluntly. Did he, or did he not, mean to try that tobacco? I dare say I was a little brusque; but it must be remembered that I had come all the way from the Inn at considerable inconvenience to give the tobacco a thorough trial.

As is the way with men of Pettigrew's type, when you corner them, he attempted to put the blame on me. "Why had I not tried the tobacco," he asked, "instead of taking a third cigar?" For reply, I asked bitingly whether that was not his third cigar. He admitted it was; but said that he smoked more quickly than I did, as if that put his behaviour in a more favourable light. I smoked my third cigar very slowly, not because I wanted to put off the experiment; for, as every one must have noted, I was most anxious to try it, but just to see what would happen. When Pettigrew had finished his cigar — and I thought he would never be done with it — he gazed at the garden-tobacco for a time, and then took a pipe from the mantelpiece. He held it first in one hand, then in the other, and then he brightened up and said that he would clean his pipes. This he did very slowly. When he had cleaned all his pipes he again looked at the garden-tobacco, which I pushed toward him. He glared at me as if I had not been doing a friendly thing, and then said, in an apologetic manner, that he would smoke a pipe until my cigar was finished. I said, " All right " cordially, thinking that he now meant to begin the experiment; but conceive my feelings when he produced a jar of the Arcadia Mixture. He filled his pipe with this and proceeded to light it, looking at me defiantly. His excuse about waiting till I had finished was too pitiful to take notice of. I finished my cigar in a few minutes, and now was the time when I would have liked to begin the experiment. As Pettigrew's guest, however, I could not take that liberty, though he impudently pushed the garden-tobacco towards me. I produced my pipe, my intention being only to half fill it with Arcadia, so that Pettigrew and I might finish our pipes at the same time. Custom, however, got the better of me, and inadvertently I filled my pipe, only noticing this when it was too late to remedy the mistake. Pettigrew thus finished before me; and though I advised him to begin on the garden-tobacco without waiting for me, he insisted on smoking half a pipeful of Arcadia, just to keep me company. It was an extraordinary thing that, try as we might, we could not finish our pipes at the same time.

About 2 a.m. Pettigrew said something about going to bed; and I arose and put down my pipe. We stood looking at the fireplace for a time, and he expressed regret that I had to leave so early in the morning. Then he put out two of the lights, and after that we both looked at the garden-tobacco. He seemed to have a sudden idea; for rather briskly he tied the tobacco up into a neat paper parcel and handed it to me, saying that I would perhaps give it a trial at the Inn. I took it without a word, but opening my hand suddenly I let it fall. My first impulse was to pick it up; but then it struck me that Pettigrew had not noticed what had happened, and that, were he to see me pick it up, he might think that I had not taken sufficient care of it. So I let it lie, and, bidding him good-night, went off to bed. I was at the foot of the stair when I thought that, after all, I should like the tobacco, so I returned. I could not see the package anywhere, but something was fizzing up the chimney, and Pettigrew had the tongs in his hand. He muttered something about his wife taking up wrong notions. Next morning that lady was very satirical about our having smoked the whole two ounces.

CHAPTER XXII

HOW HEROES SMOKE

On a tiger-skin from the ice-clad regions of the sunless North recline the heroes of Ouida, rose-scented cigars in their mouths; themselves gloriously indolent and disdainful, but, perhaps, huddled a little too closely together on account of the limited accommodation. Strathmore is here. But I never felt sure of Strathmore. Was there not less in him than met the eye? His place, Whiteladies, was a home for kings and queens; but he was not the luxurious, magnanimous creature he feigned to be. A host may be known by the cigars he keeps; and, though it is perhaps a startling thing to say, we have good reason for believing that Strathmore did not buy good cigars. I question very much whether he had many Havannahs even of the second quality at Whiteladies; if he had, he certainly kept them locked up. Only once does he so much as refer to them when at his own place, and then in the most general and suspicious way. " Bah!" he exclaims to a friend, " there is Phil smoking these wretched musk-

150

scented cigarettes again; they are only fit for Lady
Georgie or Eulalie Papellori. What taste, when
there are my Havannahs and Cheroots!" The remark, in whatever way considered, is suggestive.
In the first place, it is made late in the evening,
after Strathmore and his friend have left the smoking-room. Thus it is a safe observation. I would
not go so far as to say that he had no Havannahs
in the house; the likelihood is that he had a few in
his cigar-case, kept there for show rather than use.
These, if I understand the man, would be a good
brand but of small size — perhaps Reinas — and
they would hardly be of a well-known crop. In
colour they would be dark — say maduro — and
he would explain that he bought them because he
liked full-flavoured weeds. Possibly he had a Villar y Villar box with six or eight in the bottom of
it; but boxes are not cigars. What he did pro-
vide his friends with was Manillas. He smoked
them himself; and how careful he was of them is
seen on every other page. He is constantly stopping in the middle of his conversation to " curl a
loose leaf round his Manilla;" when one would have
expected a hero like Strathmore to fling away a
cigar when its leaves began to untwist, and light
another. So thrifty is Strathmore that he even
laboriously " curls the leaves round his cigarettes " — he does not so much as pretend that they
are Egyptian: nay, even when quarrelling with

Errol, his beloved friend (whom he shoots through the heart), he takes a cigarette from his mouth and " winds a loosened leaf " round it.

If Strathmore's Manillas were Capitan Generals they would cost him about 24s. a hundred. The probability, however, is that they were of inferior quality: say 17s. 6d. It need hardly be said that a good Manilla does not constantly require to have its leaves " curled." When Errol goes into the garden to smoke he has every other minute to " strike a fusee; " from which it may be inferred that his cigar frequently goes out. This is in itself suspicious. Errol, too, is more than once seen by his host wandering in the grounds at night with a cigar between his teeth. Strathmore thinks his susceptible friend has a love affair on hand; but is it not at least as probable an explanation that Errol had a private supply of cigars at Whiteladies, and from motives of delicacy did not like to smoke them in his host's presence? Once, indeed, we do see Strathmore smoking a good cigar, though we are not told how he came by it. When talking of the Vavasour, he " sticks his penknife through his Cabana," with the object, obviously, of smoking it to the bitter end. Another lady novelist, who is also an authority on tobacco, Miss Rhoda Broughton, contemptuously dismisses a claimant for the heroship of one of her stories, as the kind of man who turns up his trousers at the foot. It would have been just as withering to say that he stuck a penknife through his cigars.

There is another true hero with me, whose creator has unintentionally misrepresented him. It is he of " Comin' thro' the Rye," a gentleman whom the maidens of the nineteenth century will not willingly let die. He is grand, no doubt; and yet the more one thinks about him the plainer it becomes that had the heroine married him she would have been bitterly disenchanted. In her company he was magnanimous, god-like, prodigal; but in his smoking-room he showed himself in his true colours. Every lady will remember the scene where he rushes to the heroine's home and implores her to return with him to the bedside of his dying wife. The sudden announcement that his wife — whom he had thought in a good state of health — is dying, is surely enough to startle even a miser out of his niggardliness, much less a hero; and yet what do we find Vasher doing? The heroine, in frantic excitement, has to pass through his smoking-room, and on the table she sees — what? " A half-smoked cigar." He was in the middle of it when a servant came to tell him of his wife's dying request; and, before hastening to execute her wishes, he carefully laid what was left of his cigar upon the table — meaning of course to relight it when he came back. Though she did not think so, our heroine's father was a much more remarkable man

153

than Vasher. He "blew out long, comfortable
clouds" that made the whole of his large family
"cough and wink again." No ordinary father
could do that.

Among my smoking-room favourites is the hero
of Miss Adeline Sergeant's story, "Touch and
Go." He is a war correspondent; and when he
sees a body of the enemy bearing down upon him
and the wounded officer whom he has sought to
save, he imperturbably offers his companion a
cigar. They calmly smoke on while the foe
gallop up. There is something grand in this,
even though the kind of cigar is not mentioned.

I see a bearded hero, with slouch hat and shepherd's crook, a clay pipe in his mouth. He is a
Bohemian — ever a popular type of hero; and the
Bohemian is to be known all the world over by
the pipe which he prefers to a cigar. The tall
scornful gentleman who leans lazily against the
door "blowing great clouds of smoke into the air"
is the hero of a hundred novels. That is how he
is always standing when the heroine, having need
of something she has left in the drawing-room,
glides down the stairs at night in her dressing-
gown (her beautiful hair, released from its ribbons,
streaming down her neck and shoulders), and
comes most unexpectedly upon him. He is young.
The senior, over whose face "a smile flickers for
a moment" when the heroine says something naïve,

HOW HEROES SMOKE

and whom she (entirely misunderstanding her feelings) thinks she hates, smokes unostentatiously;
but though a little inclined to quiet "chaff," he is
a man of deep feeling. By and by he will open
out and gather her up in his arms. The scorner's
chair is filled. I see him, shadow-like, a sad-eyed
blasé gentleman, who has been adored by all the
beauties of fifteen seasons, and yet speaks of woman
with a contemptuous sneer. Great, however, is
love; and the vulgar little girl who talks slang
will prove to him in our next volume that there is
still one peerless beyond all others of her sex.
Ah, a wondrous thing is love. On every side of
me there are dark, handsome men, with something
sinister in their smile, "casting away their cigars
with a muffled curse." No novel would be complete without them. When they are foiled by
the brave girl of the narrative, it is the recognized
course with them to fling away their cigars with a
muffled curse. Any kind of curse would do;
but muffled ones are preferred.

CHAPTER XXIII

THE GHOST OF CHRISTMAS EVE

A few years ago, as some may remember, a startling ghost paper appeared in the monthly organ of the Society for Haunting Houses. The writer guaranteed the truth of his statement, and even gave the name of the Yorkshire manor-house in which the affair took place. The article and the discussion to which it gave rise agitated me a good deal, and I consulted Pettigrew about the advisability of clearing up the mystery. The writer wrote that he " distinctly saw his arm pass through the apparition and come out at the other side," and indeed I still remember his saying so next morning. He had a scared face, but I had presence of mind to continue eating my rolls and marmalade as if my briar had nothing to do with the miraculous affair.

Seeing that he made a " paper " of it, I suppose he is justified in touching up the incidental details. He says, for instance, that we were told the story of the ghost which is said to haunt the house, just before going to bed. As far as I remember, it was only mentioned at luncheon, and then sceptically. Instead of there being snow falling outside and an eerie wind wailing through the skeleton trees, the night was still and muggy. Lastly, I did not know, until the journal reached my hands, that he was put into the room known as the Haunted Chamber, nor that in that room the fire is noted for casting weird shadows upon the walls. This, however, may be so. The legend of the manor-house ghost he tells precisely as it is known to me. The tragedy dates back to the time of Charles I., and is led up to by a pathetic love-story, which I need not give. Suffice it that for seven days and nights the old steward had been anxiously await- ing the return of his young master and mistress from their honeymoon. On Christmas Eve, after he had gone to bed, there was a great clanging of the door-bell. Flinging on a dressing-gown, he hastened downstairs. According to the story, a number of servants watched him, and saw by the light of his candle that his face was an ashy white. He took off the chains of the door, unbolted it, and pulled it open. What he saw no human be- ing knows; but it must have been something awful, for without a cry the old steward fell dead in the hall. Perhaps the strangest part of the story is this: that the shadow of a burly man, holding a pistol in his hand, entered by the open door, stepped over the steward's body, and, gliding up the stairs, disappeared, no one could say where. Such is the legend. I shall not tell the many ingenious explanations of it that have been offered. Every Christmas Eve, however, the silent scene is said to be gone through again; and tradition declares that no person lives for twelve months at whom the ghostly intruder points his pistol.

On Christmas Day the gentleman who tells the tale in the scientific journal created some sensation at the breakfast-table by solemnly asserting that he had seen the ghost. Most of the men present scouted his story, which may be condensed into a few words. He had retired to his bedroom at a fairly early hour, and as he opened the door his candle-light was blown out. He tried to get a light from the fire, but it was too low, and eventually he went to bed in the semi-darkness. He was awakened — he did not know at what hour — by the clanging of a bell. He sat up in bed, and the ghost-story came in a rush to his mind. His fire was dead, and the room was consequently dark; yet by and by he knew, though he heard no sound, that his door had opened. He cried out, " Who is that?" but got no answer. By an effort he jumped up and went to the door, which was ajar. His bedroom was on the first floor, and looking up the stairs he could see nothing. He felt a cold sensation at his heart, however, when he looked the other way. Going slowly and without a sound down the stairs, was an old man in a dressing-gown. He carried a candle. From the top of the stairs only part of the hall is visible, but as the apparition disappeared the watcher had the courage to go down a few steps after him. At first nothing was to be seen, for the candle-light had vanished. A dim light, however, entered by the long narrow windows which flank the hall-door, and after a moment the onlooker could see that the hall was empty. He was marvelling at this sudden disappearance of the steward, when, to his horror, he saw a body fall upon the hall-floor within a few feet of the door. The watcher cannot say whether he cried out, nor how long he stood there trembling. He came to himself with a start as he realized that something was coming up the stairs. Fear prevented his taking flight, and in a moment the thing was at his side. Then he saw indistinctly that it was not the figure he had seen descend. He saw a younger man in a heavy overcoat, but with no hat on his head. He wore on his face a look of extravagant triumph. The guest boldly put out his hand towards the figure. To his amazement his arm went through it. The ghost paused for a moment and looked behind it. It was then the watcher realized that it carried a pistol in its right hand. He was by this time in a highly-strung condition, and he stood trembling lest the pistol should be

pointed at him. The apparition, however, rapidly
glided up the the stairs and was soon lost to sight.
Such are the main facts of the story; none of
which I contradicted at the time.

I cannot say absolutely that I can clear up this
mystery; but my suspicions are confirmed by a
good deal of circumstantial evidence. This will
not be understood unless I explain my strange in-
firmity. Wherever I went I used to be troubled
with a presentiment that I had left my pipe behind. Often even at the dinner-table I paused
in the middle of a sentence as if stricken with sudden pain. Then my hand went down to my
pocket. Sometimes, even after I felt my pipe, I
had a conviction that it was stopped, and only by
a desperate effort did I keep myself from produc-
ing it and blowing down it. I distinctly remember once dreaming three nights in succession that
I was on the Scotch express without it. More
than once, I know, I have wandered in my sleep,
looking for it in all sorts of places, and after I
went to bed I generally jumped out, just to make
sure of it. My strong belief, then, is that I
was the ghost seen by the writer of the paper. I
fancy that I rose in my sleep, lighted a candle and
wandered down to the hall to feel if my pipe was
safe in my coat, which was hanging there. The
light had gone out when I was in the hall. Probably the body seen to fall on the hall floor was

some other coat which I had flung there to get more easily at my own. I cannot account for the bell; but perhaps the gentleman in the Haunted Chamber dreamt that part of the affair. I had put on the overcoat before reascending; indeed, I may say that next morning I was surprised to find it on a chair in my bedroom, also to notice that there were several long streaks of candle-grease on my dressing-gown. I conclude that the pistol, which gave my face such a look of triumph, was my briar, which I found in the morning beneath my pillow. The strangest thing of all, perhaps, is that when I awoke there was a smell of tobacco-smoke in the bedroom.

CHAPTER XXIV

NOT THE ARCADIA

THOSE who do not know the Arcadia may have a mixture that their uneducated palate loves, but they are always ready to try other mixtures. The Arcadian, however, will never help himself from an outsider's pouch. Nevertheless, there was one black week when we all smoked the ordinary tobaccos. Owing to a terrible oversight on the part of our purveyor, there was no Arcadia to smoke.

We ought to have put our pipes aside and existed on cigars; but the pipes were old friends, and desert them we could not. Each of us bought a different mixture, but they tasted alike and were equally abominable. I fell ill. Doctor Southwick, knowing no better, called my malady by a learned name, but I knew to what I owed it. Never shall I forget my delight when Jimmy broke into my room one day with a pound tin of the Arcadia. Weak though I was I opened my window, and seizing the half-empty packet of tobacco that had made me ill, hurled it into the street. The tobacco scattered before it fell, but I sat at the window gloating over the packet, which lay a dirty scrap of paper, where every cab might pass over it. What I call the street is more strictly a square, for my windows were at the back of the Inn, and their view was somewhat plebeian. The square is the meeting-place of five streets, and at the corner of each the paper was caught up in a draught that bore it along to the next.

Here, it may be thought, I gladly forgot the cause of my troubles, but I really watched the paper for days. My doctor came in while I was still staring at it, and instead of prescribing more medicine he made a bet with me. It was that the scrap of paper would disappear before the dissolution of the Government. I said it would be fluttering around after the Government was dissolved, and if I lost the doctor was to get a new stethoscope. If I won my bill was to be accounted discharged. Thus, strange as it seemed, I had now cause to take a friendly interest in paper that I had previously loathed. Formerly the sight of it made me miserable; now I dreaded losing it. But I looked for it when I rose in the morning, and I could tell at once by its appearance what kind of night it had passed. Nay, more: I believe I was able to decide how the wind had been since sundown, whether there had been much traffic, and if the fire-engine had been out. There is a fire station within view of the windows, and the paper had a specially crushed appearance if the heavy engine ran over it. However, though I felt certain that I could pick my scrap of paper out of a thousand scraps, the doctor insisted on making sure. The bet was consigned to writing on the very piece of paper that suggested it. The doctor went out and captured it himself. On the back of it the conditions of the wager were formally drawn up and signed by both of us. Then we opened the window, and the paper was cast forth again. The doctor solemnly promised not to interfere with it; and I gave him a convalescent's word of honour to report progress honestly.

Several days elapsed, and I no longer found time heavy on my hands. My attention was divided between two papers, the scrap in the square and my daily copy of the *Times*. Any morning the one might tell me that I had lost my bet, or the other that I had won it; and I hurried to the window fearing that the paper had migrated to another square, and hoping my *Times* might contain the information that the Government was out. I felt that neither could last very much longer. It was remarkable how much my interest in politics had increased since I made this wager.

The doctor, I believe, relied chiefly on the scavengers. He thought they were sure to pounce upon the scrap soon. I did not, however, see why I should fear them. They came into the square

164

so seldom, and stayed so short a time when they did come, that I disregarded them. If the doctor knew how much they kept away he might say I bribed them. But perhaps he knew their ways. I got a fright one day from a dog. It was one of those low-looking animals that infest the square occasionally in half-dozens, but seldom alone. It ran up one of the side-streets, and before I realized what had happened it had the paper in its mouth. Then it stood still and looked round. For me that was indeed a trying moment. I stood at the window. The impulse seized me to fling open the sash and shake my fist at the brute; but luckily I remembered in time my promise to the doctor. I question if man was ever so interested in a mongrel before. At one of the street-corners there was a house to let, being meantime, as I had reason to believe, in the care of the wife of a police-constable. A cat was often to be seen coming up from the area to lounge in the doorway. To that cat I firmly believe I owe it that I did not then lose my wager. Faithful animal! it came up to the door: it stretched itself; in the act of doing so it caught sight of the dog, and put up its back. The dog, resenting this demonstration of feeling, dropped the scrap of paper and made for the cat. I sank back into my chair.

There was a greater disaster to be recorded next day. A working man in the square, looking about him for a pipelight, espied the paper frisking near the kerbstone. He picked it up with the obvious intention of lighting it at the stove of a wandering vendor of hot chestnuts who had just crossed the square. The working man followed, twisting the paper as he went, when — good luck again! — a young butcher almost ran into him, and the loafer, with true presence of mind, at once asked him for a match. At any rate a match passed between them; and, to my infinite relief, the paper was flung away.

I concealed the cause of my excitement from William John. He nevertheless wondered to see me run to the window every time the wind seemed to be rising, and getting anxious when it rained. Seeing that my health prevented my leaving the house, he could not make out why I should be so interested in the weather. Once I thought he was fairly on the scent. A sudden blast of wind had caught up the paper and whirled it high in the air. I may have uttered an ejaculation, for he came hurrying to the window. He found me pointing unwittingly to what was already a white speck sailing to the roof of the fire station. " Is it a pigeon?" he asked. I caught at the idea. "Yes, a carrier-pigeon," I murmured in reply; "they sometimes, I believe, send messages to the fire stations in that way." Coolly as I said this, I was conscious of grasping the window-sill in

pure nervousness till the scrap began to flutter back into the square.

Next it was squeezed between two of the bars of a drain. That was the last I saw of it, and the following morning the doctor had won his stethoscope — only by a few hours, however, for the Government's end was announced in the evening papers. My defeat discomfited me for a little, but soon I was pleased that I had lost. I would not care to win a bet over any mixture but the Arcadia.

CHAPTER XXV

A FACE THAT HAUNTED MARRIOT

"This is not a love affair," Marriot shouted, apologetically.

He had sat the others out again, but when I saw his intention I escaped into my bedroom, and now refused to come out.

"Look here," he cried, changing his tone, "if you don't come out, I'll tell you all about it through the key-hole. It is the most extraordinary story, and I can't keep it to myself. On my word of honour it isn't a love affair — at least, not exactly."

I let him talk after I had gone to bed.

"You must know," he said, dropping cigarette ash on to my pillow every minute, "that some time ago I fell in with Jack Goring's father, Colonel Goring. Jack and I had been David and Jonathan at Cambridge, and though we had not met for years I looked forward with pleasure to meeting him again. He was a widower, and his father and he kept joint house. But the house was dreary now, for the Colonel was alone in it. Jack

168

was off on a scientific expedition to the Pacific; all
the girls had been married for years. After dinner
my host and I had rather a dull hour in the
smoking-room. I could not believe that Jack
had grown very stout. 'I'll show you his photograph,' said the Colonel. An album was brought
down from a dusty shelf, and then I had to admit
that my old friend had become positively corpu-
lent. But it is not Jack I want to speak about. I
turned listlessly over the pages of the album, stopping suddenly at the face of a beautiful girl. You
are not asleep, are you?

" I am not naturally sentimental, as you know,
and even now I am not prepared to admit that I
fell in love with this face. It was not, I think, that
kind of attraction. Possibly I should have passed
the photograph by had it not suggested old times
to me — old times with a veil over them, for I
could not identify the face. That I had at some
period of my life known the original I felt certain,
but I tapped my memory in vain. The lady was
a lovely blonde, with a profusion of fair hair, and
delicate features that were Roman when they were
not Greek. To describe a beautiful woman is altogether beyond me. No doubt this face had
faults. I fancy, for instance, that there was little
character in the chin, and that the eyes were
'melting' rather than expressive. It was a vig-
nette, the hands being clasped rather fancifully at

the back of the head. My fingers drummed on the album as I sat there pondering; but when or where I had met the original I could not decide. The Colonel could give me no information. The album was Jack's, he said, and probably had not been opened for years. The photograph, too, was an old one: he was sure it had been in the house long before his son's marriage, so that (and here the hard-hearted old gentleman chuckled) it could no longer be like the original. As he seemed inclined to become witty at my expense, I closed the album, and soon afterwards I went away. I say, wake up.

"From that evening the face haunted me. I do not mean that it possessed me to the exclusion of everything else, but at odd moments it would rise before me, and then I fell into a reverie. You must have noticed my thoughtfulness of late. Often I have laid down my paper at the club and tried to think back to the original. She was probably better known to Jack Goring than to myself. All I was sure of was that she had been known to both of us. Jack and I had first met at Cambridge. I thought over the ladies I had known there; especially those who had been friends of Goring's. Jack had never been a 'lady's man' precisely; but, as he used to say, comparing himself with me, 'he had a heart.' The annals of our Cambridge days were searched in vain. I tried the country house in which he and I had spent a good many of our vacations. Suddenly I remembered the reading-party in Devonshire — but no, she was dark. Once Jack and I had a romantic adventure in Glencoe in which a lady and her daughter were concerned. We tried to make the most of it; but in our hearts we knew, after we had seen her by the morning light, that the daughter was not beautiful. Then there was the French girl at Algiers. Jack had kept me hanging on in Algiers a week longer than we meant to stay. The pose of the head, the hands clasped behind it, a trick so irritatingly familiar to me — was that the French girl? No, the lady I was struggling to identify was certainly English. I'm sure you're asleep.

"A month elapsed before I had an opportunity of seeing the photograph again. An idea had struck me which I meant to carry out. This was to trace the photograph by means of the photographer. I did not like, however, to mention the subject to Colonel Goring again, so I contrived to find the album while he was out of the smoking-room. The number of the photograph and the address of the photographer were all I wanted; but just as I had got the photograph out of the album my host returned. I slipped the thing quickly into my pocket, and he gave me no chance of replacing it. Thus it was owing to an accident that I carried the photograph away. My theft rendered me no assistance. True, the photographer's name and address were there; but when I went to the place mentioned it had disappeared to make way for 'residential chambers.' I have a few other Cambridge friends here, and I showed some of these the photograph. One, I am now aware, is under the impression that I am to be married soon; but the others were rational. Grierson, of the War Office, recognized the portrait at once. 'She is playing small parts at the Criterion,' he said. Finchley, who is a promising man at the Bar, also recognized her. 'Her portraits were in all the illustrated papers five years ago,' he told me, 'at the time when she got twelve months.' They contradicted each other about her, however; and I satisfied myself that she was neither an actress at the Criterion nor the adventuress of 1883. It was, of course, conceivable that she was an actress; but if so her face was not known in the fancy stationers' windows. Are you listening?

"I saw that the mystery would remain unsolved until Jack's return home; and when I had a letter from him a week ago, asking me to dine with him to-night, I accepted eagerly. He was just home, he said, and I would meet an old Cambridge man. We were to dine at Jack's club, and I took the photograph with me. I recognized Jack as soon as I entered the waiting-room of the club. A very short, very fat, smooth-faced man was sitting beside him with hands clasped behind his head. I believe I gaped. 'Don't you remember Tom Rufus,' Jack asked, 'who used to play the female parts at the Cambridge A.D.C.? Why, you helped me to choose his wig at Fox's. I have a photograph of him in costume somewhere at home. You might recall him by his trick of sitting with his hands clasped behind his head.' I shook Rufus's hand. I went in to dinner, and probably behaved myself. Now that it is over I cannot help being thankful that I did not ask Jack for the name of the lady before I saw Rufus. Good-night. I think I've burned a hole in the pillow."

CHAPTER XXVI

ARCADIANS AT BAY

I HAVE said that Jimmy spent much of his time contributing to various leading waste-paper baskets, and that of an evening he was usually to be found prone on my hearthrug. When he entered my room he was ever willing to tell us what he thought of editors, but his meerschaum with the cherry-wood stem gradually drove all passion from his breast, and instead of upbraiding more successful men than himself, he then lazily scribbled letters to them on my wall-paper. The wall to the right of the fireplace was thick with these epistles, which seemed to give Jimmy relief, though William John had to scrape and scrub at them next morning with india-rubber. Jimmy's sarcasm — to which that wall-paper can probably still speak — generally took this form : —

To G. BUCKLE, ESQ., *Columbia Road, Shoreditch.*

SIR, — I am requested by Mr. James Moggridge, editor of the *Times*, to return you the enclosed seven manuscripts, and to express his regret that there is at present no vacancy in the sub-editorial department of the *Times* such as Mr. Buckle kindly offers to fill.— Yours faithfully,

P. R. (for J. Moggridge, Ed. *Times*.)

To Mr. JAMES KNOWLES, *Brick Lane, Spitalfields.*

DEAR SIR,— I regret to have to return the enclosed paper, which is not quite suitable for the *Nineteenth Century*. I find that articles by unknown men, however good in themselves, attract little attention. I enclose list of contributors for next month, including, as you will observe, seven members of upper circles, and remain your obedient servant,

J. MOGGRIDGE, Ed. *Nineteenth Century*.

To Mr. W. POLLOCK, *Mile-End Road, Stepney.*

SIR,— I have on two previous occasions begged you to cease sending daily articles to the *Saturday*. Should this continue we shall be reluctantly compelled to take proceedings against you. Why don't you try the *Sporting Times?* — Yours faithfully,

J. MOGGRIDGE, Ed. *Saturday Review*.

To Messrs. SAMPSON, LOW, AND Co., *Peabody Buildings, Islington.*

DEAR SIRS,— The manuscript which you forwarded for our consideration has received careful

175

attention; but we do not think it would prove a success, and it is therefore returned to you herewith. We do not care to publish third-rate books.— We remain, yours obediently,

J. Moggridge and Co.
(late Sampson, Low, and Co.)

To H. Quilter, Esq., *P. O., Bethnal Green.*

Sir,— I have to return your paper on Universal Art. It is not without merit; but I consider art such an important subject that I mean to deal with it exclusively myself. With thanks for kindly appreciation of my new venture, I am yours faithfully,

J. Moggridge, Ed. *Universal Review.*

To John Morley, Esq., *Smith Street, Blackwall.*

Sir,— Yes, I distinctly remember meeting you on the occasion to which you refer, and it is naturally gratifying to me to hear that you enjoy my writings so much. Unfortunately, however, I am unable to accept your generous offer to do Lord Beaconsfield for the " English Men of Letters " Series, as the volume has been already arranged for.— Yours sincerely,

J. Moggridge,
Ed. " English Men of Letters " Series.

ARCADIANS AT BAY

To F. C. Burnand, Esq., *Peebles, N. B.*

Dear Sir,— The jokes which you forwarded to *Punch* on Monday last are so good that we used them three years ago.— Yours faithfully,

J. Moggridge, Ed. *Punch.*

To Mr. D'Oyley Carte, *Cross-stone Buildings, Westminster Bridge Road.*

Dear Sir,— The comic opera by your friends Messrs. Gilbert and Sullivan, which you have submitted to me, as sole lessee and manager of the Savoy Theatre, is now returned to you unread. The little piece, judged from its title-page, is bright and pleasing; but I have arranged with two other gentlemen to write my operas for the next twenty-one years.— Faithfully yours,

J. Moggridge,
Sole Lessee and Manager, Savoy Theatre.

To James Ruskin, Esq., *Railway Station Hotel, Willesden.*

Sir,— I warn you that I will not accept any more copies of your books. I do not know the individual named Tennyson to whom you refer; but if he is the scribbler who is perpetually sending me copies of his verses, please tell him that I read no poetry except my own. Why can't you leave me alone ?

J. Moggridge, Poet Laureate.

These letters of Jimmy's remind me of our famous competition, which took place on the night of the Jubilee celebrations. When all the rest of London (including William John) was in the streets the Arcadians met as usual, and Scrymgeour, at my request, put on the shutters to keep out the din. It so happened that Jimmy and Gilray were that night in wicked moods, for Jimmy, who was so anxious to be a journalist, had just had his seventeenth article returned from the *St. John's Gazette*, and Gilray had been "slated" for his acting of a new part in all the leading papers. They were now disgracing the tobacco they smoked by quarrelling about whether critics or editors were the more disreputable class, when in walked Pettigrew, who had not visited us for months. Pettigrew is as successful a journalist as Jimmy is unfortunate, and the pallor of his face showed how many Jubilee articles he had written during the past two months. Pettigrew offered each of us a Splendidad (his wife's new brand), which we dropped into the fireplace. Then he filled my little Remus with Arcadia, and sinking weariedly into a chair, said: —

"My dear Jimmy, the curse of journalism is not that editors won't accept our articles, but that they want too many from us."

This seemed such monstrous nonsense to

Jimmy that he turned his back on Pettigrew, and Gilray broke in with a diatribe against critics.

"Critics," said Pettigrew, "are to be pitied rather than reviled."

Then Gilray and Jimmy had a common foe. Whether it was Pettigrew's appearance among us or the fireworks outside that made us unusually talkative that night I cannot say, but we became quite brilliant, and when Jimmy began to give us his dream about killing an editor, Gilray said that he had a dream about criticizing critics; and Pettigrew, not to be outdone, said that he had a dream of what would become of him if he had to write any more Jubilee articles. Then it was that Marriot suggested a competition. " Let each of the grumblers," he said, " describe his dream, and the man whose dream seems the most exhilarating will get from the judges a Jubilee poundtin of the Arcadia." The grumblers agreed, but each wanted the others to dream first. At last Jimmy began as follows : —

CHAPTER XXVII

JIMMY'S DREAM

I SEE before me (said Jimmy, savagely) a court, where I, James Moggridge, am arraigned on a charge of assaulting the editor of the *St. John's Gazette*, so as to cause death. Little interest is manifested in the case. On being arrested I had pleaded guilty, and up to to-day it had been anticipated that the matter would be settled out of court. No apology, however, being forthcoming, the law has to take its course. The defence is that the assault was fair comment on a matter of public interest, and was warranted in substance and in fact. On making his appearance in the dock the prisoner is received with slight cheering.

Mr. John Jones is the first witness called for the prosecution. He says: I am assistant editor of the *St. John's Gazette*. It is an evening newspaper of pronounced Radical views. I never saw the prisoner until to-day, but I have frequently communicated with him. It was part of my work to send him back his articles. This often kept me late.

JIMMY'S DREAM!

In cross-examination the witness denies that he has ever sent the prisoner other people's articles by mistake. Pressed, he says he may have done so once. The defendant generally enclosed letters with his articles, in which he called attention to their special features. Sometimes these letters were of a threatening nature, but there was nothing unusual in that.

Cross-examined: The letters were not what he would call alarming. He had not thought of taking any special precautions himself. Of course, in his position, he had to take his chance. So far as he could remember, it was not for his own sake that the prisoner wanted his articles published, but in the interests of the public. He (the prisoner) was vexed, he said, to see the paper full of such inferior matter. Witness had frequently seen letters to the editor from other disinterested contributors couched in similar language. If he was not mistaken, he saw a number of these gentlemen in court. (Applause from the persons referred to.)

Mr. Snodgrass says: I am a poet. I do not compose during the day. The strain would be too great. Every evening I go out into the streets and buy the latest editions of the evening journals. If there is anything in them worthy commemoration in verse, I compose. There is generally something. I cannot say to which paper I send most of my poems, as I send to all. One of the weaknesses of the *St. John's Gazette* is its poetry. It is not worthy of the name. It is doggerel. I have sought to improve it, but the editor rejected my contributions. I continued to send them in the hope that they would educate his taste. One night I had sent him a very long poem which did not appear in the paper next day. I was very indignant, and went straight to the office. That was on Jubilee Day. I was told that the editor had left word that he had just gone into the country for two days. (Hisses.) I forced my way up the stairs, however, and when I reached the top I did not know which way to go. There were a number of doors with "No admittance" printed on them. (More hissing.) I heard voices in altercation in a room near me. I thought that was likely to be the editor's. I opened the door and went in. The prisoner was in the room. He had the editor on the floor and was jumping on him. I said, "Is that the editor?" He said, "Yes." I said, "Have you killed him?" He said, "Yes," again. I said, "Oh!" and went away. That is all I remember of the affair.

Cross-examined: It did not occur to me to interfere. I thought very little of the affair at the time. I think I mentioned it to my wife in the evening; but I will not swear to that. I am not the Herr Bablerr who compelled his daughter to marry a man she did not love, so that I might write an ode in celebration of the nuptials. I have no daughter. I am a poet.

The foreman-printer deposes to having had his attention called to the murder of the editor about three o'clock. He was very busy at the time. About an hour afterwards he saw the body and put a placard over it. He spoke of the matter to the assistant editor who suggested that they had better call in the police. That was done.

A clerk in the counting-house says : I distinctly remember the afternoon of the murder. I can recall it without difficulty, as it was on the following evening that I went to the theatre — a rare occurrence with me. I was running up the stairs when I met a man coming down. I recognize the prisoner as that man. He said, "I have killed your editor." I replied, "Then you ought to be ashamed of yourself." We had no further conversation.

J. O'Leary is next called. He says : I am an Irishman by birth. I had to fly my country when an iniquitous Coercion Act was put in force. At present I am a journalist, and I write Fenian leaders for the *St. John's Gazette*. I remember the afternoon of the murder. It was the sub-editor who told me of it. He asked if I would write a " par " on the subject for the fourth edition. I did so ; but as I was in a hurry to catch a train it was only a few lines. We did him fuller justice next day.

Cross-examined, witness denies that he felt any elation on hearing that a new topic had been supplied for writing on. He was sorry rather.

A policeman gives evidence that about half-past four on Jubilee Day he saw a small crowd gathered round the entrance to the offices of the *St. John's Gazette*. He thought it his duty to inquire into the matter. He went inside and asked an office-boy what was up. The boy said he thought the editor had been murdered, but advised him to inquire upstairs. He did so, and the boy's assertion was confirmed. He came down again and told the crowd that it was the editor who had been killed. The crowd then dispersed.

A detective from Scotland Yard explains the method of the prisoner's capture. Moggridge wrote to the superintendent saying that he would be passing Scotland Yard on the following Wednesday on business. Three detectives, including witness, were told off to arrest him, and they succeeded in doing so. (Loud and prolonged applause.)

The judge interposes here. He fails, he says, to see that this evidence is relevant. So far as he can see, the question is not whether a murder has been committed, but whether, under the circumstances, it is a criminal offence. The prisoner should never have been tried here at all. It was a case for the petty sessions. If the counsel cannot give some weighty reason for proceeding with further evidence, he will now put it to the jury.

After a few remarks from the counsel for the prosecution and the counsel for the defence, who calls attention to the prisoner's high and unblemished character, the judge sums up. It is for the jury, he says, to decide whether the prisoner has committed a criminal offence. That was the point; and in deciding it the jury should bear in mind the desirability of suppressing merely vexatious cases. People should not go to law over trifles. Still, the jury must remember that, without exception, all human life was sacred. After some further remarks from the judge, the jury (who deliberate for rather more than three-quarters of an hour) return a verdict of Guilty. The prisoner is sentenced to a fine of five florins, or three days' imprisonment.

CHAPTER XXVIII

GILRAY'S DREAM

CONCEIVE me (said Gilray with glowing face) invited to write a criticism of the Critics' Dramatic Society for the *Standard*. I select the *Standard* because that paper has treated me most cruelly. However, I loathe them all. My dream is the following criticism :—

What is the Critics' Dramatic Society? We found out on Wednesday afternoon, and, as we went to Drury Lane in the interests of the public, it is only fair that the public should know too. Besides, in that case we can all bear it together. Be it known, then, that this Dramatic Society is composed of " critics " who gave " The School for Scandal " at a *matinée* on Wednesday, just to show how the piece should be played. Mr. Augustus Harris had " kindly put the theatre at their disposal," for which he will have to answer when he joins Sheridan in the Elysian Fields. As the performance was by far the worst ever perpetrated, it would be a shame to deprive the twentieth century of the programme. Some of the players, as will be seen, are too well known to escape obloquy. The others may yet be able to slink into oblivion.

Sir Peter Teazle	Mr. JOHN RUSKIN.
Joseph Surface	Mr. W. E. HENLEY.
Charles Surface	Mr. HARRY LABOUCHERE.
Crabtree	Mr. W. ARCHER.
Sir Benjamin Backbite	Mr. CLEMENT SCOTT.
Moses	Mr. WALTER SICHEL.
Old Rowley	Mr. JOSEPH KNIGHT.
Sir Oliver	Mr. W. H. POLLOCK.
Trip	Mr. G. A. SALA.
Snake	Mr. MOY THOMAS.
Sir Harry Bumper (with song)	Mr. GEORGE MOORE.
Servants, guests, &c	Messrs. SAVILE CLARKE, JOSEPH HATTON, PERCY FITZGERALD, &c.

Assisted by

Lady Teazle	Miss ROSIE LE DENE.
Mrs. Candour	Miss JENNY MONTALBAN.
Lady Sneerwell	Miss ROSALIND LABELLE (The Hon. Mrs. Major TURNLEY.)
Maria	Miss JONES.

It was a sin of omission on the part of the Critics' Dramatic Society not to state that the piece played was "a new and original comedy" in many acts. Had they had the courage to do this, and to change the title, no one would ever have known. On the other hand, it was a sin of commission to allow that Professor Henry Morley was responsible for the stage-management; Mr. Morley being a man of letters whom some worthy people respect. But perhaps sins of omission and commission counter-balance. The audience was put in a bad humour before the performance began, owing to the curtain's rising fifteen minutes late. However, once the curtain did rise it was an unconscionable time in falling. What is known as the "business" of the first act, including the caterwauling of Sir Benjamin Backbite and Crabtree in their revolutions round Joseph, was gone through with a deliberation that was cruelty to the audience, and just when the act seemed over at last these indefatigable amateurs began to dance a minuet. A sigh ran round the theatre at this — a sigh as full of suffering as when a minister, having finished his thirdly and lastly, starts off again with, "I cannot allow this opportunity to pass." Possibly the Critics' Dramatic Society are congratulating themselves on the undeniable fact that the sighs and hisses grew beautifully less as the performance proceeded. But that was because the audience diminished too. One man cannot be expected to sigh like twenty; though, indeed, some of the audience of Wednesday sighed like at least half a dozen.

If it be true that all men — even critics — have their redeeming points and failings, then was there no Charles and no Joseph Surface at this unique *matinée*. For the ungainly gentleman who essayed

the part of Charles made, or rather meant to make,
him spotless; and Mr. Henley's Joseph was twin-
brother to Mr. Irving's Mephistopheles. Perhaps
the idea of Mr. Labouchere and his friend, Mr.
Henley, was that they would make one young
man between them. They found it hard work.
Mr. Labouchere has yet to learn that buffoonery
is not exactly wit, and that Charles Surfaces who
dig their Uncle Olivers in the ribs and then turn to
the audience for applause are among the things
that the nineteenth century can do without. According to the programme, Mr. George Moore
— the Sir Harry Bumper — was to sing the song,
" Here's to the Maiden of Bashful Fifteen." Mr.
Moore did not sing it, but Mr. Labouchere did.
The explanation of this, we understand, was not
that Sir Harry's heart failed him at the eleventh
hour, but that Mr. Labouchere threatened to fling
up his part unless the song was given to him.
However, Mr. Moore heard Mr. Labouchere singing the song, and that was revenge enough for any
man. To Mr. Henley the part of Joseph evidently presented no serious difficulties. In his
opinion, Joseph is a whining hypocrite who rolls
his eyes when he wishes to look natural. Obviously he is a slavish admirer of Mr. Irving. If
Joseph had taken his snuff as this one does, Lady
Sneerwell would have sent him to the kitchen. If
he had made love to Lady Teazle as this one

does, she would have suspected him of weak intellect. Sheridan's Joseph was a man of culture: Mr. Henley's is a buffoon. It is not, perhaps, so much this gentleman's fault as his misfortune that his acting is without either art or craft; but then he was not compelled to play Joseph Surface. Indeed, we may go further, and say that if he is a man with friends he must have been dissuaded from it. The Sir Peter Teazle of Mr. Ruskin reminded us of other Sir Peter Teazles — probably because Sir Peter is played nowadays with his courtliness omitted.

Mr. William Archer was the Crabtree, or rather Mr. Archer and the prompter between them. Until we caught sight of the prompter we had credited Mr. Archer with being a ventriloquist given to casting his voice to the winds. Mr. Clement Scott — the Sir Benjamin Backbite — was a ventriloquist too, but not in such a large way as Mr. Archer. His voice, so far as we could make out from an occasional rumble, was in his boots, where his courage kept it company. There was no more ambitious actor in the cast than Mr. Pollock. Mr. Pollock was Sir Oliver, and he gave a highly original reading of that old gentleman. What Mr. Pollock's private opinion of the character of Sir Oliver may be we cannot say; it would be worth an interviewer's while to find out. But if he thinks Sir Oliver was a windmill, we can in-

form him at once that he is mistaken. Of Mr
Sichel's Moses all that occurs to us to say is, that
when he let his left arm hang down and raised
the other aloft he looked very like a teapot. Mr.
Joseph Knight was Old Rowley. In that character all we saw of him was his back; and we are
bound to admit that it was unexceptionable. Sheridan calls one of his servants Snake, and the other
Trip. Mr. Moy Thomas tried to look as like a
snake as he could, and with some success. The
Trip of Mr. Sala, however, was a little heavy, and
when he came between the audience and the other
actors there was a temporary eclipse. As for the
minor parts, the gentlemen who personated them
gave a capital rendering of supers suffering from
stage-fever. Wednesday is memorable in the history of the stage; but we would forget it if we
could.

CHAPTER XXIX

PETTIGREW'S DREAM

My dream (said Pettigrew) contrasts sadly with those of my young friends. They dream of revenge, but my dream is tragic. I see my editor writing my obituary notice. This is how it reads:—

Mr. Pettigrew, M.A., whose sad death is recorded in another column, was in his forty-second year (not his forty-fourth, as stated in the evening papers), and had done a good deal of Jubilee work before he accepted the commission that led to his death. It is an open secret that he wrote seventy of the Jubilee sketches which have appeared in this paper. The pamphlet now selling in the streets for a penny, entitled "Jubilees of the Past," was his. He wrote the introductory chapter to "Fifty Years of Progress," and his "Jubilee Statesmen" is now in a second edition. The idea of a collection of Jubilee odes was not his but the publishers. At the same time his friends and relatives attach no blame to them. Mr. Pettigrew shivered when the order was given to him, but he accepted it, and the general impression among those who knew him was that a man who had survived "Jubilee Statesmen" could do anything. As it turns out we had over-estimated Mr. Pettigrew's powers of endurance.

As "The Jubilee Odes" will doubtless yet be collected by another hand, little need be said here of the work. Mr. Pettigrew was to make his collection as complete as the limited space at his disposal (two volumes) would allow; the only original writing in the book being a sketch of the various schemes suggested for the celebration of the Jubilee. It was this sketch that killed him. On the morning of the 27th, when he intended beginning it, he rose at an unusually early hour, and was seen from the windows of the house pacing the garden in an apparently agitated state of mind. He ate no breakfast. One of his daughters states that she noticed a wild look in his eyes during the morning meal; but, as she did not remark on it at the time, much stress need not be laid on this. The others say that he was unusually quiet and silent. All, however, noticed one thing. Generally, when he had literary work to do, he was anxious to begin upon his labours, and spent little time at the breakfast-table. On this occasion he sat on. Even after the breakfast-things were removed he seemed reluctant to adjourn to the study. His wife asked him several times if he meant to begin "The Jubilee Odes" that day, and he always replied in the affirmative. But he talked nervously of other things; and, to her surprise — though she thought comparatively little of it at the time — drew her on to a discussion on summer bonnets. As a rule, this was a subject which he shunned. At last he rose, and, going slowly to the window, looked out for a quarter of an hour. His wife asked him again about "The Jubilee Odes," and he replied that he meant to begin directly. Then he went round the morning-room, looking at the pictures on the walls as if for the first time. After that he leant for a little while against the mantelpiece, and then, as if an idea had struck him, began to wind up the clock. He went through the house winding up the clocks though this duty was usually left to a servant; and when that was over he came back to the breakfast-room and talked about Waterbury watches. His wife had to go to the kitchen, and he followed her. On their way back they passed the nursery, and he said he thought he would go in and talk to the nurse. This was very unlike him. At last his wife said that it would soon be luncheon-time, and then he went to the study. Some ten minutes afterwards he wandered into the dining-room, where she was arranging some flowers. He seemed taken aback at seeing her, but said, after a moment's thought, that the study door was locked and he could not find the key.

This astonished her, as she had dusted the room herself that morning. She went to see, and found the study door standing open. When she returned to the dining-room he had disappeared. They searched for him everywhere, and eventually discovered him in the drawing-room, turning over a photograph album. He then went back to the study. His wife accompanied him, and, as was her custom, filled his pipe for him. He smoked a mixture to which he was passionately attached. He lit his pipe several times, but it always went out. His wife put a new nib into his pen, placed some writing material on the table, and then retired, shutting the door behind her.

About half an hour afterwards Mrs. Pettigrew sent one of the children to the study on a trifling errand. As he did not return she followed him. She found him sitting on his father's knee, where she did not remember ever having seen him before. Mr. Pettigrew was holding his watch to the boy's ears. The study table was littered with several hundreds of Jubilee odes. Other odes had slipped to the floor. Mrs. Pettigrew asked how he was getting on, and her unhappy husband replied that he was just going to begin. His hands were trembling, and he had given up trying to smoke. He sought to detain her by talking about the boy's curls; but she went away, taking the child with her. As she closed the door he groaned

heavily, and she reopened it to ask if he felt unwell. He answered in the negative, and she left
him. The last person to see Mr. Pettigrew alive
was Eliza Day, the housemaid. She took a letter
to him between twelve and one o'clock. Usually
he disliked being disturbed at his writing; but
this time, in answer to her knock, he cried eagerly,
"Come in!" When she entered he insisted on
her taking a chair, and asked her how her people
were, and if there was anything he could do for
them. Several times she rose to leave, but he
would not allow her to do so. Eliza mentioned
this in the kitchen when she returned to it. Her
master was naturally a reserved man who seldom
spoke to his servants, which rendered his behaviour
on this occasion the more remarkable.

As announced in the evening papers yesterday,
the servant sent to the study at half-past one to
see why Mr. Pettigrew was not coming to lunch,
found him lifeless on the floor. The knife clutched
in his hand showed that he had done the fatal
deed himself; and Dr. Southwick, of Hyde Park,
who was on the spot within ten minutes of the
painful discovery, is of opinion that life had been
extinct for about half an hour. The body was
lying among Jubilee odes. On the table were a
dozen or more sheets of "copy," which, though
only spoiled pages, showed that the deceased had
not succumbed without a struggle. On one he

had begun, " Fifty years have come and gone since a fair English maiden ascended the throne of England." Another stopped short at, " To every loyal Englishman the Jubil———." A third sheet commenced with, " Though there have been a number of royal Jubilees in the history of the world, probably none has awakened the same interest as ——— " and a fourth began, " 1887 will be known to all future ages as the year of Jub——— " One sheet bore the sentence, " Heaven help me ! " and it is believed that these were the last words the deceased ever penned.

Mr. Pettigrew was a most estimable man in private life, and will be greatly missed in the circles to which he had endeared himself. He leaves a widow and a small family. It may be worth adding that when discovered dead there was a smile upon his face, as if he had at last found peace. He must have suffered great agony that forenoon, and his death is best looked upon as a happy release.

Marriot, Scrymgeour and I awarded the tin of Arcadia to Pettigrew because he alone of the competitors seemed to believe that his dream might be realized.

CHAPTER XXX

THE MURDER IN THE INN

SOMETIMES I think it is all a dream, and that I did not really murder the waits. Perhaps they are living still. Yet the scene is very vivid before me, though the affair took place — if it ever did take place — so long ago that I cannot be expected to remember the details. The time when I must give up smoking was drawing near, so that I may have been unusually irritable, and determined, whatever the cost, to smoke my last pound-tin of the Arcadia in peace. I think my briar was in my mouth when I did it, but after the lapse of months I cannot say whether there were three of them or only two. So far as I can remember I took the man with the beard first.

The incident would have made more impression on me had there been any talk about it. So far as I could discover, it never got into the papers. The porters did not seem to think it any affair of theirs, though one of them must have guessed why I invited the waits upstairs. He saw me open the door to them; he was aware that this was their third visit in a week; and only the night before he had heard me shout a warning to them from my Inn window. But of course the porters must allow themselves a certain discretion in the performance of their duties. Then there was the pleasant gentleman of the next door but two, who ran against me just as I was toppling the second body over the railing. We were not acquainted, but I knew him as the man who had flung a water-jug at the waits the night before. He stopped short when he saw the body (it had rolled out of the sofa-rug), and looked at me suspiciously. "He is one of the waits," I said. "I beg your pardon," he replied, "I did not understand." When he had passed a few yards he turned round. "Better cover him up," he said, "or people will talk." Then he strolled away, an air from "The Grand Duchess" lightly trolling from his lips. We still meet occasionally, and nod if no one is looking.

I am going too fast, however. What I meant to say was that the murder was premeditated. In the case of a reprehensible murder I know this would be considered an aggravation of the offence. Of course it is an open question whether all murders are not reprehensible; but let that pass. To my own mind I should have been indeed deserving of punishment had I rushed out and slain the waits in a moment of fury. If one were to give way to his passion every time he is interrupted in his work or his sleep by bawlers our thoroughfares would soon be choked with the dead. No one values human life or understands its sacredness more than I do. I merely say that there may be times when a man, having stood a great deal and thought it over calmly, is justified in taking the law into his own hands — always supposing he can do it decently, quietly, and without scandal. The epidemic of waits broke out early in December, and every other night or so these torments came in the still hours and burst into song beneath my windows. They made me nervous. I was more wretched on the nights they did not come than on the nights they came; for I had begun to listen for them, and was never sure they had gone into an-other locality before four o'clock in the morning. As for their songs, they were more like music-hall ditties than Christmas carols. So one morning — it was, I think, the 23rd of December — I warned them fairly, fully, and with particulars, of what would happen if they disturbed me again. Hav-ing given them this warning, can it be said that I was to blame — at least to any considerable extent?

Christmas Eve had worn into Christmas morn-ing before the waits arrived on that fateful occa-sion. I opened the window — if my memory does not deceive me — at once, and looked down at them. I could not swear to their being the persons whom I had warned the night before. Perhaps I should have made sure of this. But in any case these were practiced waits. Their whine rushed in at my open window with a vigour that proved them no tyros. Besides, the night was a cold one and I could not linger at an open casement. I nodded pleasantly to the waits, and pointed to my door. Then I ran downstairs and let them in. They came up to my chambers with me. As I have said, the lapse of time prevents my remembering how many of them there were: three I fancy. At all events, I took them into my bedroom and strangled them one by one. They went off quite peaceably; the only difficulty was in the disposal of the bodies. I thought of laying them on the kerbstone or in different passages; but I was afraid the police might not see that they were waits, in which case I might be put to inconvenience. So I took a spade and dug two (or three) large holes in the quadrangle of the Inn. Then I carried the bodies to the place in my rug one at a time, shoved them in, and covered them up. A close observer might have noticed in that part of the quadrangle, for some time after, a small mound, such as might be made by an elbow under the bed-clothes. Nobody, however, seems to have descried it, and yet I see it often even now in my dreams.

CHAPTER XXXI

THE PERILS OF NOT SMOKING

When the Arcadians heard that I had signed an agreement to give up smoking they were first incredulous, then sarcastic, then angry. Instead of coming as usual to my room they went one night in a body to Pettigrew's, and there, as I afterwards discovered, a scheme for "saving me" was drawn up. So little did they understand the firmness of my character that they thought I had weakly yielded to the threats of the lady referred to in my first chapter, when, of course, I had only yielded to her arguments, and they agreed to make an appeal on my behalf to her. Pettigrew, as a married man himself, was appointed intercessor, and I understand that the others not only accompanied him to her door but waited in an alley until he came out. I never knew whether the reasoning brought to bear on the lady was of Pettigrew's devising or suggested by Jimmy and the others, but it was certainly unselfish of Pettigrew to lie so freely on my account. At the time, however, the plot enraged me, for the lady conceived the absurd idea that I had sent Pettigrew to her.

Undoubtedly it was a bold stroke. Pettigrew's scheme was to play upon his hostess's attachment for me by hinting to her that if I gave up smoking I would probably die. Finding her attentive rather than talkative, he soon dared to assure her that he himself loathed tobacco and only took it for his health.

"By the doctor's orders, mark you," he said, impressively, "Dr. Southwick, of Hyde Park."

She expressed polite surprise at this, and then Pettigrew, believing he had made an impression, told his story as concocted.

"My own case," he said, "is one much in point. I suffered lately from sore throat, accompanied by depression of spirits and loss of appetite. The ailment was so unusual with me that I thought it prudent to put myself in Dr. Southwick's hands. As far as possible I shall give you his exact words:

"'When did you give up smoking?' he asked, abruptly, after examining my throat.

"'Three months ago,' I replied, taken by surprise, 'but how did you know I had given it up?'

"'Never mind how I know,' he said, severely; 'I told you that, however much you might desire to do so, you were not to take to not smoking. This is how you carry out my directions.'

203

" ' Well,' I answered, sulkily, ' I have been feeling so healthy for the last two years that I thought I could indulge myself a little. You are aware how I abominate tobacco.'

" ' Quite so,' he said, ' and now you see the result of this miserable self-indulgence. Two years ago I prescribed tobacco for you, to be taken three times a day, and you yourself admit that it made a new man of you. Instead of feeling thankful, you complain of the brief unpleasantness that accompanies its consumption, and now in the teeth of my instructions you give it up. I must say the ways of patients are a constant marvel to me.'

" ' But how,' I asked, ' do you know that my reverting to the pleasant habit of not smoking is the cause of my present ailment ? '

" ' Oh ! ' he said, ' you are not sure of that yourself, are you ? '

" ' I thought,' I replied, ' there might be a doubt about it; though of course I have not forgotten what you told me two years ago.'

" ' It matters very little,' he said, ' whether you remember what I tell you if you do not follow my orders. But as for knowing that indulgence in not smoking is what has brought you to this state, how long is it since you noticed these symptoms ? '

" ' I can hardly say,' I answered. ' Still I should be able to think back. I had my first sore throat this year the night I saw Mr. Irving at the Lyceum, and that was on my wife's birthday, the 3rd of October. How long ago is that?'

" 'Why, that is more than three months ago. Are you sure of the date?'

" 'Quite certain,' I told him; 'so you see I had my first sore throat before I risked not smoking again.'

" 'I don't understand this,' he said. 'Do you mean to say that in the beginning of May you were taking my prescription daily? You were not missing a day now and then—forgetting to order a new stock of cigars when the others were done, or flinging them away before they were half smoked? Patients do such things.'

" 'No, I assure you I compelled myself to smoke. At least ——'

" 'At least what? Come, now, if I am to be of any service to you, there must be no reserve.'

" 'Well, now that I think of it, I was only smoking one cigar a day at that time.'

" 'Ah! we have it now,' he cried. 'One cigar a day, when I ordered you three. I might have guessed as much. When I tell non-smokers that they must smoke or I will not be answerable for the consequences, they entreat me to let them break themselves of the habit of not smoking gradually. One cigarette a day to begin with, they beg of me, promising to increase the dose by degrees. Why, man, one cigarette a day is poison; it is worse than not smoking.'

" ' But that is not what I did.'

" ' The idea is the same,' he said. ' Like the others, you make all this moan about giving up completely a habit you should never have acquired. For my own part, I cannot even understand where the subtle delights of not smoking come in. Compared with health, they are surely immaterial?'

" ' Of course, I admit that.'

" 'Then, if you admit it, why pamper yourself?'

" ' I suppose because one is weak in matters of habit. You have many cases like mine?'

" ' I have such cases every week,' he told me; ' indeed, it was having so many cases of the kind that made me a specialist in the subject. When I began practice I had not the least notion how common the non-tobacco throat, as I call it, is.'

" ' But the disease has been known, has it not, for a long time?'

" ' Yes,' he said; ' but the cause has only been discovered recently. I could explain the malady to you scientifically, as many medical men would prefer to do; but you are better to have it in plain English.'

" ' Certainly; but I should like to know whether the symptoms in other cases have been in every way similar to mine.'

THE PERILS OF NOT SMOKING

" ' They have doubtless differed in degree, but not otherwise,' he answered. ' For instance, you say your sore throat is accompanied by depression of spirits.'

" ' Yes; indeed the depression sometimes precedes the sore throat.'

" ' Exactly. I presume, too, that you feel most depressed in the evening — say, immediately after dinner?'

" ' That is certainly the time I experience the depression most.'

" ' The result,' he said, ' if I may venture on somewhat delicate matters, is that your depression of spirits infects your wife and family, even your servants?'

" ' That is quite true,' I answered. ' Our home has by no means been so happy as formerly. When a man is out of spirits, I suppose, he tends to be brusque and undemonstrative to his wife, and to be easily irritated by his children. Certainly that has been the case with me of late.'

" ' Yes,' he exclaimed, ' and all because you have not carried out my directions. Men ought to see that they have no right to indulge in not smoking, if only for the sake of their wives and families. A bachelor has more excuse, perhaps; but think of the example you set your children in not making an effort to shake this self-indulgence off. In short, smoke for the sake of your wife

MY LADY NICOTINE

and family if you won't smoke for the sake of your health.' "

I think this is pretty nearly the whole of Pettigrew's story, but I may add that he left the house in depression of spirits, and then infected Jimmy and the others with the same ailment, so that they should all have hurried in a cab to the house of Dr. Southwick.

" Honestly," Pettigrew said, " I don't think she believed a word I told her."

" If she had only been a man," Marriot sighed, " we could have got round her."

" How ? " asked Pettigrew.

" Why, of course," said Marriot, " we could have sent her a tin of the Arcadia."

CHAPTER XXXII

MY LAST PIPE

THE night of my last smoke drew near without any demonstration on my part or on that of my friends. I noticed that none of them was now comfortable if left alone with me, and I knew, I cannot tell how, that though they had too much delicacy to refer in my presence to my coming happiness, they often talked of it among themselves. They smoked hard, and looked covertly at me, and had an idea that they were helping me. They also addressed me in a low voice, and took their seats noiselessly, as if some one were ill in the next room.

"We have a notion," Scrymgeour said, with an effort, on my second last night, "that you would rather we did not feast you to-morrow evening?"

"Oh, I want nothing of that kind," I said.

"So I fancied," Jimmy broke in. "Those things are rather a mockery, but of course if you thought it would help you in any way ——"

"Or if there is anything else we could do for you," interposed Gilray, "you have only to mention it."

Though they irritated rather than soothed me, I was touched by their kindly intentions, for at one time I feared my friends would be sarcastic. The next night was my last, and I found that they had been looking forward to it with genuine pain. As will have been seen, their custom was to wander into my room one by one, but this time they came together. They had met in the boudoir, and came up the stair so quietly that I did not hear them. They all looked very subdued, and Marriot took the cane-chair so softly that it did not creak. I noticed that after a furtive glance at me, each of them looked at the centre table, on which lay my briar, Romulus and Remus, three other pipes that all had their merits, though they never touched my heart until now, my clay tobacco-jar, and my old pouch. I had said good-bye to these before my friends came in, and I could now speak with a comparatively firm voice. Marriot and Gilray and Scrymgeour signed to Jimmy, as if some plan of action had been arranged, and Jimmy said huskily, sitting upon the hearthrug:

"Pettigrew isn't coming. He was afraid he would break down."

Then we began to smoke. It was as yet too early in the night for my last pipe, but soon I regretted that I had not arranged to spend this night alone. Jimmy was the only one of the Arcadians who had been at school with me, and he was full of reminiscences which he addressed to the others just as if I was not present.

"He was the life of the old school," Jimmy said, referring to me, "and when I shut my eyes I can hear his merry laugh as if we were both in knicker-bockers still."

"What sort of character did he have among the fellows?" Gilray whispered.

"The very best. He was the soul of honour, and we all anticipated a great future for him. Even the masters loved him; indeed, I question if he had an enemy."

"I remember my first meeting with him at the University," said Marriot, "and that I took to him at once. He was speaking at the Debating Society that night, and his enthusiasm quite carried me away."

"And how we shall miss him here," said Scrymgeour, "and in my house-boat. I think I had better sell the house-boat. Do you remember his favourite seat at the door of the saloon?"

"Do you know," said Marriot, looking a little scared, "I thought I would be the first of our lot to go. Often I have kept him up late in this very room talking of my own troubles, and little guessing why he sometimes treated them a little testily."

So they talked, meaning very well, and by and by it struck one o'clock. A cold shiver passed through me, and Marriot jumped from his chair. It had been agreed that I should begin my last pipe at one precisely.

Whatever my feelings were up to this point I had kept them out of my face, but I suppose a change came over me now. I tried to lift my briar from the table, but my hand shook and the pipe tapped, tapped on the deal like an auction-eer's hammer.

"Let me fill it," Jimmy said, and he took my old briar from me. He scraped it energetically so that it might hold as much as possible, and then he filled it. Not one of them, I am glad to remember, proposed a cigar for my last smoke, or thought it possible that I would say farewell to tobacco through the medium of any other pipe than my briar. I liked my briar best. I have said this already, but I must say it again. Jimmy handed the briar to Gilray, who did not surrender it until it reached my mouth. Then Scrymgeour made a spill, and Marriot lit it. In another mo-ment I was smoking my last pipe. The others glanced at each other, hesitated, and put their pipes into their pockets.

There was little talking, for they all gazed at me as if something astounding might happen at any moment. The clock had stopped, but the ventilator was clicking. Although Jimmy and the others saw only me, I tried not to see only them. I conjured up the face of a lady, and she smiled encouragingly, and then I felt safer. But at times her face was lost in smoke, or suddenly it was Marriot's face, eager, doleful, wistful.

At first I puffed vigorously and wastefully, then I became scientific and sent out rings of smoke so strong and numerous that half a dozen of them were in the air at a time. In past days I had often followed a ring over the table, across chairs, and nearly out at the window, but that was when I blew one by accident and was loth to let it go. Now I distributed them among my friends, who let them slip away into the looking-glass. I think I had almost forgotten what I was doing and where I was, when an awful thing happened. My pipe went out.

" There are remnants in it yet," Jimmy cried, with forced cheerfulness, while Gilray blew the ashes off my sleeve, Marriot slipped a cushion behind my back, and Scrymgeour made another spill. Again I smoked, but no longer recklessly.

It is revealing no secret to say that a drowning man sees his whole past unfurl before him like a panorama. So little, however, was I, now on the eve of a great happiness, like a drowning man, that nothing whatever passed before me. I lost sight even of my friends, and though Jimmy was on his knees at my feet, his hand clasping mine, he disappeared as if his open mouth had swallowed

the rest of his face. I had only one thought—
that I was smoking my last pipe. Unconsciously
I crossed my legs, and one of my slippers fell off.
Jimmy, I think, slipped it on to my foot. Marriot stood over me, gazing into the bowl of my
pipe, but I did not see him.

Now I was puffing tremendously, but no smoke
came. The room returned to me, I saw Jimmy
clearly, I felt Marriot overhead, and I heard them
all whispering. Still I puffed; I knew that my
pipe was empty, but still I puffed. Gilray's fingers tried to draw my briar from my mouth, but I
bit into it with my teeth, and still I puffed.

When I came to I was alone. I had a dim
consciousness of having been shaken by several
hands, of a voice that I think was Scrymgeour's
saying that he would often write to me — though
my new home was to be within the four-mile
radius — and of another voice that I think was
Jimmy's, telling Marriot not to let me see him
breaking down. But though I had ceased to
puff, my briar was still in my mouth; and, indeed, I found it there when William John shook
me into life the next morning.

My parting with William John was almost
sadder than the scene of the previous night. I
rang for him when I had tied up all my treasures
in brown paper, and I told him to give the tobacco-jar to Jimmy, Romulus to Marriot, Remus to

MY LAST PIPE

Gilray, and the pouch to Scrymgeour. William John bore up till I came to the pouch, when he fairly blubbered. I had to hurry into my bedroom, but I mean to do something yet for William John. Not even Scrymgeour knew so well as he what my pouch had been to me, and till I die I shall always regret that I did not give it to William John. I kept my briar.

CHAPTER XXXIII

WHEN MY WIFE IS ASLEEP AND ALL THE HOUSE IS STILL

PERHAPS the heading of this chapter will deceive some readers into thinking that I smoke nowadays in camera. It is, I know, a common jest among smokers that such a promise as mine is seldom kept, and I allow that the Arcadians tempt me still. But never shall it be said of me with truth that I have broken my word. I smoke no more, and, indeed, though the scenes of my bachelorhood frequently rise before me in dreams, painted as Scrymgeour could not paint them, I am glad, when I wake up, that they are only dreams. Those selfish days are done, and I see that though they were happy days, the happiness was a mistake. As for the struggle that is supposed to take place between a man and tobacco after he sees smoking in its true colours, I never experienced it. I have not even any craving for the Arcadia now, though it is a tobacco that should only be smoked by our greatest men. Were we to present a tin of it to our national heroes, instead of the freedom of the city, they would probably thank us more. Jimmy and the others are quite unworthy to smoke it; indeed, if I had my way they would give up smoking altogether. Nothing, perhaps, shows more completely how I have severed my bonds than this: that my wife is willing to let our friends smoke in the study, but I will not hear of it. There shall be no smoking in my house; and I have determined to speak to Jimmy about smoking out at our spare bedroom window. It is a mere contemptible pretence to say that none of the smoke comes back into the room. The curtains positively reek of it, and we must have them washed at once. I shall speak plainly to Jimmy because I want him to tell the others. They must understand clearly on what terms they are received in this house, and if they prefer making chimneys of themselves to listening to music, by all means let them stay at home.

But when my wife is asleep and all the house is still, I listen to the man through the wall. At such times I have my briar in my mouth, but there is no harm in that, for it is empty. I did not like to give away my briar, knowing no one who understood it, and I always carry it about with me now to remind me of my dark past. When the man through the wall lights up I put my cold pipe in my mouth and we have a quiet hour together.

I have never to my knowledge seen the man through the wall, for his door is round the corner,

and, besides, I have no interest in him until half-
past eleven p.m. We begin then. I know him
chiefly by his pipes, and them I know by his taps
on the wall as he knocks the ashes out of them.
He does not smoke the Arcadia, for his temper
is hasty, and he breaks the coals with his foot.
Though I am compelled to say that I do not consider his character very lovable he has his good
points, and I like his attachment to his briar. He
scrapes it, on the whole, a little roughly, but that
is because he is so anxious to light up again, and
I discovered long ago that he has signed an agreement with his wife to go to bed at half-past twelve.
For some time I could not understand why he had
a silver rim put on the bowl. I noticed the
change in the tap at once, and the natural conclusion would have been that the bowl had cracked.
But it never had the tap of a cracked bowl. I
was reluctant to believe that the man through the
wall was merely some vulgar fellow, and I felt
that he could not be so or else he would have
smoked his meerschaum more. At last I understood. The bowl had worn away on one side,
and the silver rim had been needed to keep the
tobacco in. Undoubtedly this was the explanation,
for even before the rim came I was a little puzzled
by the taps of the briar. He never seemed to hit
the wall with the whole mouth of the bowl, but
of course the reason was that he could not. At

the same time I do not exonerate him from blame. He is a clumsy smoker to burn his bowl at one side, and I am afraid he lets the stem slip round in his teeth. Of course I see that the mouthpiece is loose, but a piece of blotting-paper would remedy that.

His meerschaum is not such a good one as Jimmy's. Though Jimmy's boastfulness about his meerschaum was hard to bear, none of us ever denied the pipe's worth. The man through the wall has not a cherry-wood-stem to his meerschaum, and consequently it is too light. A ring has been worn into the palm of his left hand owing to his tapping the meerschaum there, and it is as marked as Jimmy's ring, for, though Jimmy tapped more strongly, the man through the wall has to tap oftener.

What I chiefly dislike about the man through the wall is his treatment of his clay. A clay, I need scarcely say, has an entirely different tap from a meerschaum, but the man through the wall does not treat these two pipes as if they were on an equality. He ought to tap his clay on the palm of his hand, but he seldom does so, and I am strongly of opinion that when he does, it is only because he has forgotten that this is not the meerschaum. Were he to tap the clay on the wall or on the ribs of the fire he would smash it, so he taps it on a coal. About this there is something contemptible.   I am not complaining because he has little affection for his clay.   In face of all that has been said in honour of clays, and knowing that this statement will occasion an outcry against me, I admit that I never cared for clays myself.   A rank tobacco is less rank through a churchwarden, but to smoke the Arcadia through a clay is to incur my contempt, and even my resentment.   But to disbelieve in clays is one thing and to treat them badly is another.   If the man through the wall has decided after reflection and experiment that his clay is a mistake, I say let him smoke it no more; but so long as he does smoke it I would have it receive consideration from him.   I very much question whether, if he read his heart, he could learn from it that he loves his meerschaum more than his clay, yet because the meerschaum cost more he taps it on his palm.   This is a serious charge to bring against any man, but I do not make it lightly.

The man through the wall smokes each of these three pipes nightly, beginning with the briar. Thus he does not like a hot pipe.   Some will hold that he ought to finish with the briar, as it is his favourite, but I am not of that opinion.   Undoubtedly, I think, the first pipe is the sweetest; indeed, I feel bound to make a statement here.   I have an uneasy feeling that I never did justice to meerschaums, and for this reason: I only smoked them after my briar was hot, so that I never gave them a fair chance. If I had begun the day with a meerschaum, might it not have shown itself in a new light? That is a point I shall never be able to decide now, but I often think of it, and I leave the verdict to others.

Even though I did not know that the man through the wall must retire at half-past twelve, his taps at that hour would announce it. He then gives each of his pipes a final tap, not briskly as before, but slowly, as if he was thinking between each tap. I have sometimes decided to send him a tin of the only tobacco to smoke, but on the whole I could not undertake the responsibility of giving a man, whom I have only studied for a few months, such a testimonial. Therefore when his last tap says good-night to me I take my cold briar out of my mouth, tap it on the mantelpiece, smile sadly, and so to bed.

MARGARET OGILVY

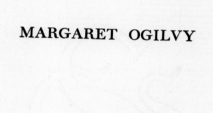

TO THE MEMORY OF
MY SISTER JANE ANN

CHAPTER I

HOW MY MOTHER GOT HER SOFT FACE

ON the day I was born we bought six hair-bottomed chairs, and in our little house it was an event, the first great victory in a woman's long campaign; how they had been laboured for, the pound-note and the thirty threepenny bits they cost, what anxiety there was about the purchase, the show they made in possession of the west room, my father's unnatural coolness when he brought them in (but his face was white) — I so often heard the tale afterwards, and shared as boy and man in so many similar triumphs, that the coming of the chairs seems to be something I remember, as if I had jumped out of bed on that first day, and run ben to see how they looked. I am sure my mother's feet were ettling to be ben long before they could be trusted, and that the moment after she was left alone with me she was discovered barefooted in the west room, doctoring a scar (which she had been the first to detect) on one of the chairs, or sitting on them regally or withdrawing and re-opening the door suddenly to take the six by surprise. And then, I think, a shawl was flung over her (it is strange to me to think it was not I who ran after her with the shawl), and she was escorted sternly back to bed and reminded that she had promised not to budge, to which her reply was probably that she had been gone but an instant, and the implication that therefore she had not been gone at all. Thus was one little bit of her revealed to me at once: I wonder if I took note of it. Neighbours came in to see the boy and the chairs. I wonder if she deceived me when she affected to think that there were others like us, or whether I saw through her from the first, she was so easily seen through. When she seemed to agree with them that it would be impossible to give me a college education, was I so easily taken in, or did I know already what ambitions burned behind that dear face? when they spoke of the chairs as the goal quickly reached, was I such a newcomer that her timid lips must say "They are but a beginning" before I heard the words? And when we were left together, did I laugh at the great things that were in her mind, or had she to whisper them to me first, and then did I put my arm round her and tell her that I would help? Thus it was for such a long time: it is strange to me to feel that it was not so from the beginning.

It is all guess-work for six years, and she whom I see in them is the woman who came suddenly into view when they were at an end. Her timid lips I have said, but they were not timid then, and when I knew her the timid lips had come. The soft face — they say the face was not so soft then. The shawl that was flung over her — we had not begun to hunt her with a shawl, nor to make our bodies a screen between her and the draughts, nor to creep into her room a score of times in the night to stand looking at her as she slept. We did not see her becoming little then, nor sharply turn our heads when she said wonderingly how small her arms had grown. In her happiest moments — and never was a happier woman — her mouth did not of a sudden begin to twitch, and tears to lie on the mute blue eyes in which I have read all I know and would ever care to write. For when you looked into my mother's eyes you knew, as if He had told you, why God sent her into the world — it was to open the minds of all who looked to beautiful thoughts. And that is the beginning and end of literature. Those eyes that I cannot see until I was six years old have guided me through life, and I pray God they may remain my only earthly judge to the last. They were never more my guide than when I helped to put her to earth, not whimpering because my mother had been taken away after seventy-six glorious years of life, but exulting in her even at the grave.

She had a son who was far away at school. I remember very little about him, only that he was a merry-faced boy who ran like a squirrel up a tree and shook the cherries into my lap. When he was thirteen and I was half his age the terrible news came, and I have been told the face of my mother was awful in its calmness as she set off to get between Death and her boy. We trooped with her down the brae to the wooden station, and I think I was envying her the journey in the mysterious waggons; I know we played around her, proud of our right to be there, but I do not recall it, I only speak from hearsay. Her ticket was taken, she had bidden us good-bye with that fighting face which I cannot see, and then my father came out of the telegraph-office and said huskily "He's gone!" Then we turned very quietly and went home again up the little brae. But I speak from hearsay no longer; I knew my mother for ever now.

That is how she got her soft face and her pathetic ways and her large charity, and why other mothers ran to her when they had lost a child. "Dinna greet, poor Janet," she would say to them, and they would answer, " Ah, Margaret, but you're greeting yoursel'." Margaret Ogilvy had been her maiden name, and after the Scotch custom she was still Margaret Ogilvy to her old friends. Margaret Ogilvy I loved to name her. Often when I was a boy, " Margaret Ogilvy, are you there ? " I would call up the stair.

She was always delicate from that hour, and for many months she was very ill. I have heard that the first thing she expressed a wish to see was the christening robe, and she looked long at it and then turned her face to the wall. That was what made me as a boy think of it always as the robe in which he was christened, but I knew later that we had all been christened in it, from the oldest of the family to the youngest, between whom stood twenty years. Hundreds of other children were christened in it also, such robes being then a rare possession, and the lending of ours among my mother's glories. It was carried carefully from house to house, as if it were itself a child; my mother made much of it, smoothed it out, petted it, smiled to it before putting it into the arms of those to whom it was being lent; she was in our pew to see it borne magnificently (something inside it now) down the aisle to the pulpit side, when a stir of expectancy went through the church and we kicked each other's feet beneath the book-board but were reverent in the face; and however the child might behave, laughing brazenly or skirling to its mother's shame, and whatever the father as he held it up might do, look doited probably and bow at the wrong time, the christening robe of long experience helped them through. And

when it was brought back to her she took it in her
arms as softly as if it might be asleep, and unconsciously pressed it to her breast: there was never
anything in the house that spoke to her quite so
eloquently as that little white robe; it was the one
of her children that always remained a baby.   And
she had not made it herself, which was the most
wonderful thing about it to me, for she seemed to
have made all other things.   All the clothes in the
house were of her making, and you don't know
her in the least if you think they were out of the
fashion; she turned them and made them new
again, she beat them and made them new again,
and then she coaxed them into being new again
just for the last time, she let them out and took
them in and put on new braid, and added a piece
up the back, and thus they passed from one member of the family to another until they reached the
youngest, and even when we were done with them
they reappeared as something else.   In the fashion!
I must come back to this.   Never was a woman
with such an eye for it.   She had no fashion-plates;
she did not need them.   The minister's wife (a
cloak), the banker's daughters (the new sleeve)—
they had but to pass our window once, and the
scalp, so to speak, was in my mother's hands.   Observe her rushing, scissors in hand, thread in mouth,
to the drawers where her daughters' Sabbath clothes
were kept.   Or go to church next Sunday, and

watch a certain family filing in, the boy lifting his legs high to show off his new boots, but all the others demure, especially the timid, unobservant looking little woman in the rear of them. If you were the minister's wife that day or the banker's daughters you would have got a shock. But she bought the christening robe, and when I used to ask why, she would beam and look conscious, and say she wanted to be extravagant once. And she told me, still smiling, that the more a woman was given to stitching and making things for herself, the greater was her passionate desire now and again to rush to the shops and " be foolish." The christening robe with its pathetic frills is over half a century old now, and has begun to droop a little, like a daisy whose time is past, but it is as fondly kept together as ever : I saw it in use again only the other day.

My mother lay in bed with the christening robe beside her, and I peeped in many times at the door and then went to the stair and sat on it and sobbed. I know not if it was that first day, or many days afterwards, that there came to me my sister, the daughter my mother loved the best, yes, more I am sure even than she loved me, whose great glory she has been since I was six years old. This sister, who was then passing out of her teens, came to me with a very anxious face and wringing her hands, and she told me to go ben to my mother and say to her that she still had another boy. I went ben excitedly, but the room was dark, and when I heard the door shut and no sound come from the bed I was afraid, and I stood still. I suppose I was breathing hard, or perhaps I was crying, for after a time I heard a listless voice that had never been listless before say, " Is that you ? " I think the tone hurt me, for I made no answer, and then the voice said more anxiously, " Is that you ? " again. I thought it was the dead boy she was speaking to, and I said in a little lonely voice, " No, it's no him, it's just me." Then I heard a cry, and my mother turned in bed, and though it was dark I knew that she was holding out her arms.

After that I sat a great deal in her bed trying to make her forget him, which was my crafty way of playing physician, and if I saw any one out of doors do something that made the others laugh I immediately hastened to that dark room and did it before her. I suppose I was an odd little figure; I have been told that my anxiety to brighten her gave my face a strained look and put a tremor into the joke (I would stand on my head in the bed, my feet against the wall, and then cry excitedly, " Are you laughing, mother ? ") — and perhaps what made her laugh was something I was unconscious of, but she did laugh suddenly now and then, whereupon I screamed exultantly to that dear sister, who was ever in waiting, to come and see the sight, but by the time she came the soft face was wet again. Thus I was deprived of some of my glory, and I remember once only making her laugh before witnesses. I kept a record of her laughs on a piece of paper, a stroke for each, and it was my custom to show this proudly to the doctor every morning. There were five strokes the first time I slipped it into his hand, and when their meaning was explained to him, he laughed so boisterously that I cried, "I wish that was one of hers!" Then he was sympathetic, and asked me if my mother had seen the paper yet, and when I shook my head he said that if I showed it to her now and told her that these were her five laughs he thought I might win another. I had less confidence, but he was the mysterious man whom you ran for in the dead of night (you flung sand at his window to waken him, and if it was only toothache he extracted the tooth through the open window, but when it was something sterner he was with you in the dark square at once, like a man who slept in his topcoat), so I did as he bade me, and not only did she laugh then but again when I put the laugh down, so that though it was really one laugh with a tear in the middle I counted it as two.

It was doubtless that same sister who told me not to sulk when my mother lay thinking of him,

but to try instead to get her to talk about him. I
did not see how this could make her the merry
mother she used to be, but I was told that if I
could not do it nobody could, and this made me
eager to begin. At first, they say, I was often
jealous, stopping her fond memories with the cry,
"Do you mind nothing about me?" but that did
not last; its place was taken by an intense desire
(again, I think, my sister must have breathed it
into life) to become so like him that even my
mother should not see the difference, and many
and artful were the questions I put to that end.
Then I practised in secret, but after a whole week
had passed I was still rather like myself. He had
such a cheery way of whistling, she had told me,
it had always brightened her at her work to hear
him whistling, and when he whistled he stood
with his legs apart, and his hands in the pockets
of his knickerbockers. I decided to trust to this,
so one day after I had learned his whistle (every
boy of enterprise invents a whistle of his own)
from boys who had been his comrades, I secretly
put on a suit of his clothes, dark grey they were,
with little spots, and they fitted me many years
afterwards, and thus disguised I slipped, unknown
to the others, into my mother's room. Quaking,
I doubt not, yet so pleased, I stood still until she
saw me, and then — how it must have hurt her!
"Listen!" I cried in a glow of triumph, and I

stretched my legs wide apart and plunged my hands into the pockets of my knickerbockers, and began to whistle.

She lived twenty-nine years after his death — such active years, until toward the end, that you never knew where she was unless you took hold of her — and though she was frail henceforth and ever growing frailer, her housekeeping again became famous, so that brides called as a matter of course to watch her ca'ming and sanding and stitching: there are old people still, one or two, to tell with wonder in their eyes how she could bake twenty-four bannocks in the hour, and not a chip in one of them. And how many she gave away, how much she gave away of all she had, and what pretty ways she had of giving it! Her face beamed and rippled with mirth as before, and her laugh, that I had tried so hard to force, came running home again. I have heard no such laugh as hers save from merry children; the laughter of most of us ages, and wears out with the body, but hers remained gleeful to the last, as if it were born afresh every morning. There was always something of the child in her, and her laugh was its voice, as eloquent of the past to me as was the christening robe to her. But I had not made her forget the bit of her that was dead; in those nine and twenty years he was not removed one day farther from her. Many a time she fell asleep speaking to him, and even while she slept her lips moved and she smiled as if he had come back to her, and when she woke he might vanish so suddenly that she started up bewildered and looked about her, and then said slowly, "My David's dead!" or perhaps he remained long enough to whisper why he must leave her now, and then she lay silent with filmy eyes. When I became a man and he was still a boy of thirteen, I wrote a little paper called "Dead this Twenty Years," which was about a similar tragedy in another woman's life, and it is the only thing I have written that she never spoke about, not even to that daughter she loved the best. No one ever spoke of it to her, or asked her if she had read it: one does not ask a mother if she knows that there is a little coffin in the house. She read many times the book in which it is printed, but when she came to that chapter she would put her hands to her heart or even over her ears.

CHAPTER II

WHAT she had been, what I should be, these were the two great subjects between us in my boyhood, and while we discussed the one we were deciding the other, though neither of us knew it.

Before I reached my tenth year a giant entered my native place in the night, and we woke to find him in possession. He transformed it into a new town at a rate with which we boys only could keep up, for as fast as he built dams we made rafts to sail in them; he knocked down houses, and there we were crying, " Pilly!" among the ruins; he dug trenches, and we jumped them; we had to be dragged by the legs from beneath his engines; he sunk wells, and in we went. But though there were never circumstances to which boys could not adapt themselves in half an hour, older folk are slower in the uptake, and I am sure they stood and gaped at the changes so suddenly being worked in our midst, and scarce knew their way home now in the dark. Where had been formerly but the click of the shuttle was soon the roar of "power," hand-looms were pushed into a corner as a room is cleared for a dance, every morning at half-past five the town was awakened with a yell, and from a chimney-stalk that rose high into our caller air the conqueror waved for evermore his flag of smoke. Another era had dawned, new customs, new fashions sprang into life, all as lusty as if they had been born at twenty-one; as quickly as two people may exchange seats, the daughter, till now but a knitter of stockings, became the breadwinner, he who had been the breadwinner sat down to the knitting of stockings; what had been yesterday a nest of weavers was to-day a town of girls.

I am not of those who would fling stones at the change; it is something, surely, that backs are no longer prematurely bent; you may no more look through dim panes of glass at the aged poor weaving tremulously for their little bit of ground in the cemetery. Rather are their working years too few now, not because they will it so, but because it is with youth that the power-looms must be fed. Well, this teaches them to make provision, and they have the means as they never had before. Not in batches are boys now sent to college, the half-dozen a year have dwindled to one, doubtless because in these days they can begin to draw wages as they step out of their fourteenth year. Here assuredly there is loss, but all the losses would be but a pebble in a sea of gain were it not for this, that with so many of the family, young mothers among them, working in the factories, home life is not so beautiful as it was. So much of what is great in Scotland has sprung from the closeness of the family ties; it is there I sometimes fear that my country is being struck. That we are all being reduced to one dead level, that "character" abounds no more and life itself is less interesting, such things I have read, but I do not believe them. I have even seen them given as my reason for writing of a past time, and in that at least there is no truth. In our little town, which is a sample of many, life is as interesting, as pathetic, as joyous as ever it was; no group of weavers was better to look at or think about than the rivulet of winsome girls that over-runs our streets every time the sluice is raised, the comedy of summer evenings and winter firesides is played with the old zest, and every window-blind is the curtain of a romance. Once the lights of a little town are lit, who could ever hope to tell all its story, or the story of a single wynd in it? And who looking at lighted windows needs to turn to books? The reason my books deal with the past instead of with the life I myself have known is simply this, that I soon grow tired of writing tales unless I can see a little girl, of whom my mother has told me, wandering confidently through the pages. Such a grip has her memory of her girlhood had upon me since I was a boy of six.

Those innumerable talks with her made her youth as vivid to me as my own, and so much more quaint, for, to a child, the oddest of things, and the most richly coloured picture-book, is that his mother was once a child also, and the contrast between what she is and what she was is perhaps the source of all humour. My mother's father, the one hero of her life, died nine years before I was born, and I remember this with bewilderment, so familiarly does the weather-beaten mason's figure rise before me from the old chair on which I was nursed and now write my books. On the surface he is as hard as the stone on which he chiselled, and his face is dyed red by its dust, he is rounded in the shoulders and a "hoast" hunts him ever; sooner or later that cough must carry him off, but until then it shall not keep him from the quarry, nor shall his chapped hands, as long as they can grasp the mell. It is a night of rain or snow, and my mother, the little girl in a pinafore who is already his housekeeper, has been many times to the door to look for him. At last he draws nigh, hoasting. Or I see him setting off to church, for he was a great "stoop" of the Auld Licht kirk, and his mouth is very firm now as if there were a case of discipline to face, but on his

way home he is bowed with pity. Perhaps his
little daughter who saw him so stern an hour ago
does not understand why he wrestles so long in
prayer to-night, or why when he rises from his
knees he presses her to him with unwonted tenderness. Or he is in this chair repeating to her
his favourite poem, " The Cameronian's Dream,"
and at the first lines so solemnly uttered,

> In a dream of the night I was wafted away,

she screams with excitement, just as I screamed
long afterwards when she repeated them in his
voice to me. Or I watch, as from a window,
while she sets off through the long parks to the
distant place where he is at work, in her hand a
flaggon which contains his dinner. She is singing
to herself and gleefully swinging the flaggon, she
jumps the burn and proudly measures the jump
with her eye, but she never dallies unless she
meets a baby, for she was so fond of babies that
she must hug each one she met, but while she
hugged them she also noted how their robes were
cut, and afterwards made paper patterns, which
she concealed jealously, and in the fullness of time
her first robe for her eldest born was fashioned
from one of these patterns, made when she was in
her twelfth year.

She was eight when her mother's death made
her mistress of the house and mother to her little

brother, and from that time she scrubbed and
mended and baked and sewed, and argued with
the flesher about the quarter-pound of beef and
penny bone which provided dinner for two days
(but if you think that this was poverty you don't
know the meaning of the word), and she carried
the water from the pump, and had her washing
days and her ironings and a stocking always on
the wire for odd moments, and gossiped like a
matron with the other women, and humoured the
men with a tolerant smile — all these things she
did as a matter of course, leaping joyful from bed
in the morning because there was so much to do,
doing it as thoroughly and sedately as if the brides
were already due for a lesson, and then rushing
out in a fit of childishness to play dumps or pa-
laulays with others of her age. I see her frocks
lengthening, though they were never very short,
and the games given reluctantly up. The horror
of my boyhood was that I knew a time would
come when I also must give up the games, and
how it was to be done I saw not (this agony still
returns to me in dreams, when I catch myself
playing marbles, and look on with cold dis-
pleasure); I felt that I must continue playing in
secret, and I took this shadow to her, when she
told me her own experience, which convinced us
both that we were very like each other inside.
She had discovered that work is the best fun after

all, and I learned it in time, but have my lapses, and so had she.

I know what was her favourite costume when she was at the age that they make heroines of: it was a pale blue with a pale blue bonnet, the white ribbons of which tied aggravatingly beneath the chin, and when questioned about this garb she never admitted that she looked pretty in it, but she did say, with blushes too, that blue was her colour, and then she might smile, as at some memory, and begin to tell us about a man who—but it ended there with another smile which was longer in departing. She never said, indeed she denied strenuously, that she had led the men a dance, but again the smile returned, and came between us and full belief. Yes, she had her little vanities; when she got the Mizpah ring she did carry that finger in such a way that the most reluctant must see. She was very particular about her gloves, and hid her boots so that no other should put them on, and then she forgot their hiding-place, and had suspicions of the one who found them. A good way of enraging her was to say that her last year's bonnet would do for this year without alteration, or that it would defy the face of clay to count the number of her shawls. In one of my books there is a mother who is setting off with her son for the town to which he had been called as minister, and she pauses on the threshold to ask him anxiously if he thinks her bonnet "sets" her. A reviewer said she acted thus, not because she cared how she looked, but for the sake of her son. This, I remember, amused my mother very much.

I have seen many weary on-dings of snow, but the one I seem to recollect best occurred nearly twenty years before I was born. It was at the time of my mother's marriage to one who proved a most loving as he was always a well-loved husband, a man I am very proud to be able to call my father. I know not for how many days the snow had been falling, but a day came when the people lost heart and would make no more gullies through it, and by next morning to do so was impossible, they could not fling the snow high enough. Its back was against every door when Sunday came, and none ventured out save a valiant few, who buffeted their way into my mother's home to discuss her predicament, for unless she was "cried" in the church that day she might not be married for another week, and how could she be cried with the minister a field away and the church buried to the waist? For hours they talked, and at last some men started for the church, which was several hundred yards distant. Three of them found a window, and forcing a passage through it, cried the pair, and that is how it came about that my father and mother were married on the first of March.

WHAT SHE HAD BEEN

That would be the end, I suppose, if it were a story, but to my mother it was only another beginning, and not the last. I see her bending over the cradle of her first-born, college for him already in her eye (and my father not less ambitious), and anon it is a girl who is in the cradle, and then another girl — already a tragic figure to those who know the end. I wonder if any instinct told my mother that the great day of her life was when she bore this child; what I am sure of is that from the first the child followed her with the most wistful eyes and saw how she needed help and longed to rise and give it. For of physical strength my mother had never very much; it was her spirit that got through the work, and in those days she was often so ill that the sand rained on the doctor's window, and men ran to and fro with leeches, and "she is in life, we can say no more" was the information for those who came knocking at the door. " I am sorrow to say," her father writes in an old letter now before me, "that Margaret is in a state that she was never so bad before in this world. Till Wednesday night she was in as poor a condition as you could think of to be alive. However, after bleeding, leeching, etc., the Dr. says this morning that he is better hoped now, but at present we can say no more but only she is alive and in the hands of Him in whose hands all our lives are. I can give you no adequate view of what my feelings are, indeed they are a burden too heavy for me and I cannot describe them. I look on my right and left hand and find no comfort, and if it were not for the rock that is higher than I my spirit would utterly fail, but blessed be His name who can comfort those that are cast down. O for more faith in His supporting grace in this hour of trial."

Then she is "on the mend," she may "thole thro'" if they take great care of her, "which we will be forward to do." The fourth child dies when but a few weeks old, and the next at two years. She was her grandfather's companion, and thus he wrote of her death, this stern, self-educated Auld Licht with the chapped hands:

"I hope you received my last in which I spoke of Dear little Lydia being unwell. Now with deep sorrow I must tell you that yesterday I assisted in laying her dear remains in the lonely grave. She died at 7 o'clock on Wednesday evening, I suppose by the time you had got the letter. The Dr. did not think it was croup till late on Tuesday night, and all that Medical aid could prescribe was done, but the Dr. had no hope after he saw that the croup was confirmed, and hard indeed would the heart have been that would not have melted at seeing what the dear little creature suffered all Wednesday until the feeble frame was quite worn out. She was quite sensible till within

WHAT SHE HAD BEEN

2 hours of her death, and then she sunk quite low till the vital spark fled, and all medicine that she got she took with the greatest readiness, as if apprehensive they would make her well. I cannot well describe my feelings on the occasion. I thought that the fountain head of my tears had now been dried up, but I have been mistaken, for I must confess that the briny rivulets descended fast on my furrowed cheeks, she was such a winning Child, and had such a regard for me and always came and told me all her little things, and as she was now speaking, some of her little prattle was very taking, and the lively images of these things intrude themselves more into my mind than they should do, but there is allowance for moderate grief on such occasions. But when I am telling you of my own grief and sorrow, I know not what to say of the bereaved Mother, she hath not met with anything in this world before that hath gone so near the quick with her. She had no handling of the last one as she was not able at the time, for she only had her once in her arms, and her affections had not time to be so fairly entwined around her. I am much afraid that she will not soon if ever get over this trial. Although she was weakly before, yet she was pretty well recovered, but this hath not only affected her mind but her body is so much affected that she is not well able to sit so long as her bed is making and hath

scarcely tasted meat [i. e. food] since Monday night, and till some time is elapsed we cannot say how she may be. There is none that is not a parent themselves that can fully sympathise with one in such a state. David is much affected also, but it is not so well known on him, and the younger branches of the family are affected but it will be only momentary. But alas in all this vast ado, there is only the sorrow of the world which worketh death, O how gladdening would it be if we were in as great bitterness for sin as for the loss of a first-born. O how unfitted persons or families is for trials who knows not the divine art of casting all their cares upon the Lord, and what multitudes are there that when earthly comforts is taken away, may well say what have I more? all their delight is placed in some one thing or another in the world, and who can blame them for unwillingly parting with what they esteem their chief good. O that we were wise to lay up treasure for the time of need, for it is truly a solemn affair to enter the lists with the king of terrors. It is strange that the living lay the things so little to heart until they have to engage in that war where there is no discharge. O that my head were waters and mine eyes a fountain of tears that I might weep day and night for my own and others' stupidity in this great matter. O for grace to do every day work in its proper time and to live above the tempting cheating train of earthly things. The rest of the family are moderately well. I have been for some days worse than I have been for 8 months past, but I may soon get better, I am in the same way I have often been in before, but there is no security for it always being so, for I know that it cannot be far from the time when I will be one of those that once were. I have no other news to send you, and as little heart for them. I hope you will take the earliest opportunity of writing that you can, and be particular as regards Margaret, for she requires consolation."

He died exactly a week after writing this letter, but my mother was to live for another forty-four years. And joys of a kind never shared in by him were to come to her so abundantly, so long drawn out, that, strange as it would have seemed to him to know it, her fuller life had scarce yet begun. And with the joys were to come their sweet, frightened comrades, pain and grief, again she was to be touched to the quick, again and again to be so ill that " she is in life, we can say no more," but still she had attendants very " forward " to help her, some of them unborn in her father's time.

She told me everything, and so my memories of our little red town are coloured by her memories. I knew it as it had been for generations, and suddenly I saw it change, and the transformation could not fail to strike a boy, for these first years are the most impressionable (nothing that happens after we are twelve matters very much); they are also the most vivid years when we look back, and more vivid the farther we have to look, until, at the end, what lies between bends like a hoop, and the extremes meet. But though the new town is to me a glass through which I look at the old, the people I see passing up and down these wynds, sitting, night-capped, on their barrow-shafts, hobbling in their blacks to church on Sunday, are less those I saw in my childhood than their fathers and mothers who did these things in the same way when my mother was young. I cannot picture the place without seeing her, as a little girl, come to the door of a certain house and beat her bass against the gav'le-end, or there is a wedding tonight, and the carriage with the white-eared horse is sent for a maiden in pale blue, whose bonnet-strings tie beneath the chin.

CHAPTER III

MY mother was a great reader, and with ten minutes to spare before the starch was ready would
begin the "Decline and Fall" — and finish it, too,
that winter. Foreign words in the text annoyed
her and made her bemoan her want of a classical
education—she had only attended a Dame's school
during some easy months—but she never passed
the foreign words by until their meaning was explained to her, and when next she and they met it
was as acquaintances, which I think was clever of
her. One of her delights was to learn from me
scraps of Horace, and then bring them into her
conversation with "colleged men." I have come
upon her in lonely places, such as the stair-head or
the east room, muttering these quotations aloud to
herself, and I well remember how she would say
to the visitors, "Ay, ay, it's very true, Doctor, but
as you know, 'Eheu fugaces, Postume, Postume,
labuntur anni,'" or "Sal, Mr. so and so, my lassie
is thriving well, but would it no be more to the
point to say 'O mater, pulchra filia pulchrior'?"

251

which astounded them very much if she managed
to reach the end without being flung, but usually
she had a fit of laughing in the middle, and so
they found her out.

Biography and exploration were her favourite
reading, for choice the biography of men who had
been good to their mothers, and she liked the explorers to be alive so that she could shudder at the
thought of their venturing forth again, but though
she expressed a hope that they would have the
sense to stay at home henceforth, she gleamed with
admiration when they disappointed her.   In later
days I had a friend who was an African explorer,
and she was in two minds about him; he was one
of the most engrossing of mortals to her, she admired him prodigiously, pictured him at the head
of his caravan, now attacked by savages, now by
wild beasts, and adored him for the uneasy hours
he gave her, but she was also afraid that he
wanted to take me with him, and then she thought
he should be put down by law.   Explorers' mothers also interested her very much; the books
might tell her nothing about them, but she could
create them for herself and wring her hands in
sympathy with them when they had got no news
of him for six months.   Yet there were times when
she grudged him to them — as the day when he
returned victorious.   Then what was before her
eyes was not the son coming marching home

again, but an old woman peering for him round the window curtain and trying not to look up-lifted. The newspaper reports would be about the son, but my mother's comment was "She's a proud woman this night."

We read many books together when I was a boy, "Robinson Crusoe" being the first (and the second), and the "Arabian Nights" should have been the next, for we got it out of the library (a penny for three days), but on discovering that they were nights when we had paid for knights we sent that volume packing, and I have curled my lips at it ever since. "The Pilgrim's Progress" we had in the house (it was as common a possession as a dresser-head), and so enamoured of it was I that I turned our garden into sloughs of Despond, with pea-sticks to represent Christian on his travels and a buffet-stool for his burden, but when I dragged my mother out to see my handi-work she was scared, and I felt for days, with a certain elation, that I had been a dark character. Besides reading every book we could hire or bor-row I also bought one now and again, and while buying (it was the occupation of weeks) I read, standing at the counter, most of the other books in the shop, which is perhaps the most exquisite way of reading. And I took in a magazine called "Sunshine," the most delicious periodical, I am sure, of any day. It cost a halfpenny or a penny a month, and always, as I fondly remember, had a continued tale about the dearest girl, who sold water-cress, which is a dainty not grown and I suppose never seen in my native town. This romantic little creature took such hold of my imagination that I cannot eat water-cress even now without emotion. I lay in bed wondering what she would be up to in the next number; I have lost trout because when they nibbled my mind was wandering with her; my early life was embittered by her not arriving regularly on the first of the month. I know not whether it was owing to her loitering on the way one month to an extent flesh and blood could not bear, or because we had exhausted the penny library, but on a day I conceived a glorious idea, or it was put into my head by my mother, then desirous of making progress with her new clouty hearth-rug. The notion was nothing short of this, why should I not write the tales myself? I did write them— in the garret — but they by no means helped her to get on with her work, for when I finished a chapter I bounded downstairs to read it to her, and so short were the chapters, so ready was the pen, that I was back with new manuscript before another clout had been added to the rug. Authorship seemed, like her bannock-baking, to consist of running between two points. They were all tales of adventure (happiest is he who writes of

adventure), no characters were allowed within if
I knew their like in the flesh, the scene lay in
unknown parts, desert islands, enchanted gardens,
with knights (none of your nights) on black
chargers, and round the first corner a lady selling water-cress.

At twelve or thereabout I put the literary calling to bed for a time, having gone to a school
where cricket and football were more esteemed,
but during the year before I went to the university, it woke up and I wrote great part of a three-
volume novel. The publisher replied that the
sum for which he would print it was a hundred
and — however, that was not the important point
(I had sixpence): where he stabbed us both was
in writing that he considered me a "clever lady."
I replied stiffly that I was a gentleman, and since
then I have kept that manuscript concealed. I
looked through it lately, and, oh, but it is dull.
I defy any one to read it.

The malignancy of publishers, however, could
not turn me back. From the day on which I first
tasted blood in the garret my mind was made up;
there could be no hum-dreadful-drum profession
for me; literature was my game. It was not
highly thought of by those who wished me well.
I remember being asked by two maiden ladies,
about the time I left the university, what I was to
be, and when I replied brazenly, "An author,"

they flung up their hands, and one exclaimed reproachfully, "And you an M. A.!" My mother's
views at first were not dissimilar; for long she
took mine jestingly as something I would grow
out of, and afterwards they hurt her so that I tried
to give them up. To be a minister — that she
thought was among the fairest prospects, but she
was a very ambitious woman, and sometimes she
would add, half scared at her appetite, that there
were ministers who had become professors, " but
it was not canny to think of such things."

I had one person only on my side, an old tailor,
one of the fullest men I have known, and quite
the best talker. He was a bachelor (he told me
all that is to be known about woman), a lean man,
pallid of face, his legs drawn up when he walked,
as if he was ever carrying something in his lap;
his walks were of the shortest, from the tea-pot on
the hob to the board on which he stitched, from
the board to the hob, and so to bed. He might
have gone out had the idea struck him, but in the
years I knew him, the last of his brave life, I think
he was only in the open twice, when he "flitted"
— changed his room for another hard by. I did
not see him make these journeys, but I seem to
see him now, and he is somewhat dizzy in the odd
atmosphere; in one hand he carries a box-iron, he
raises the other, wondering what this is on his
head — it is a hat; a faint smell of singed cloth goes

by with him. This man had heard of my set of photographs of the poets and asked for a sight of them, which led to our first meeting. I remember how he spread them out on his board, and after looking long at them, turned his gaze on me and said solemnly,

> What can I do to be for ever known,
> And make the age to come my own?

These lines of Cowley were new to me, but the sentiment was not new, and I marvelled how the old tailor could see through me so well. So it was strange to me to discover presently that he had not been thinking of me at all, but of his own young days, when that couplet sang in his head, and he, too, had thirsted to set off for Grub Street, but was afraid, and while he hesitated old age came, and then Death, and found him grasping a box-iron.

I hurried home with the mouthful, but neighbours had dropped in, and this was for her ears only, so I drew her to the stair, and said imperiously,

> What can I do to be for ever known,
> And make the age to come my own?

It was an odd request for which to draw her from a tea-table, and she must have been surprised, but I think she did not laugh, and in after years she would repeat the lines fondly, with a flush on her soft face. "That is the kind you would like to be yourself!" we would say in jest to her, and she would reply almost passionately, "No, but I would be windy of being his mother." It is possible that she could have been his mother had that other son lived, he might have managed it from sheer love of her, but for my part I can smile at one of those two figures on the stair now, having long given up the dream of being for ever known, and seeing myself more akin to my friend, the tailor; for as he was found at the end on his board, so I hope shall I be found at my hand-loom, doing honestly the work that suits me best. Who shall know so well as I that it is but a hand-loom compared to the great guns that reverberate through the age to come? But she who stood with me on the stair that day was a very simple woman, accustomed all her life to making the most of small things, and I weaved sufficiently well to please her, which has been my only steadfast ambition since I was a little boy.

Not less than mine became her desire that I should have my way — but, ah, the iron seats in that Park of horrible repute, and that bare room at the top of many flights of stairs! While I was away at college she drained all available libraries for books about those who go to London to live by the pen, and they all told the same shuddering

tale. London, which she never saw, was to her a
monster that licked up country youths as they
stepped from the train; there were the garrets in
which they sat abject, and the park seats where
they passed the night. Those park seats were the
monster's glaring eyes to her, and as I go by them
now she is nearer to me than when I am in any
other part of London. I daresay that when night
comes, this Hyde Park which is so gay by day is
haunted by the ghosts of many mothers, who run,
wild-eyed, from seat to seat, looking for their sons.

But if we could dodge those dreary seats she
longed to see me try my luck, and I sought to ex-
clude them from the picture by drawing maps of
London with Hyde Park left out. London was
as strange to me as to her, but long before I was
shot upon it I knew it by maps, and drew them
more accurately than I could draw them now.
Many a time she and I took our jaunt together
through the map, and were most gleeful, popping
into telegraph offices to wire my father and sister
that we should not be home till late, winking to
my books in lordly shop-windows, lunching at
restaurants (and remembering not to call it dinner),
saying, "How do?" to Mr. Alfred Tennyson when
we passed him in Regent Street, calling at publishers' offices for a cheque, when "Will you take
care of it, or shall I?" I asked gaily, and she
would be certain to reply, " I'm thinking we'd bet-

ter take it to the bank and get the money," for she always felt surer of money than of cheques, so to the bank we went (" Two tens, and the rest in gold "), and thence straightway (by cab) to the place where you buy sealskin coats for middling old ladies. But ere the laugh was done the park would come through the map like a blot.

" If you could only be sure of as much as would keep body and soul together," my mother would say with a sigh.

" With something over, mother, to send to you."

" You couldna expect that at the start."

The wench I should have been courting now was journalism, that grisette of literature who has a smile and a hand for all beginners, welcoming them at the threshold, teaching them so much that is worth knowing, introducing them to the other lady whom they have worshipped from afar, showing them even how to woo her, and then bidding them a bright God-speed — he were an ingrate who, having had her joyous companion-ship, no longer flings her a kiss as they pass. But though she bears no ill-will when she is jilted, you must serve faithfully while you are hers, and you must seek her out and make much of her, and, until you can rely on her good-nature (note this), not a word about the other lady. When at last she took me in I grew so fond of her that I called her by the other's name, and even now I think at times that there was more fun in the little sister, but I began by wooing her with contributions that were all misfits. In an old book I find columns of notes about works projected at this time, nearly all to consist of essays on deeply uninteresting subjects; the lightest was to be a volume on the older satirists, beginning with Skelton and Tom Nash — the half of that manuscript still lies in a dusty chest — the only story was about Mary Queen of Scots, who was also the subject of many unwritten papers. Queen Mary seems to have been luring me to my undoing ever since I saw Holyrood, and I have a horrid fear that I may write that novel yet. That anything could be written about my native place never struck me. We had read somewhere that a novelist is better equipped than most of his trade if he knows himself and one woman, and my mother said, " You know yourself, for everybody must know himself" (there never was a woman who knew less about herself than she), and she would add dolefully, "But I doubt I'm the only woman you know well."

" Then I must make you my heroine," I said lightly.

" A gey auld-farrant-like heroine ! " she said, and we both laughed at the notion — so little did we read the future.

Thus it is obvious what were my qualifications when I was rashly engaged as a leader-writer (it was my sister who saw the advertisement) on an English provincial paper. At the moment I was as uplifted as the others, for the chance had come at last, with what we all regarded as a prodigious salary, but I was wanted in the beginning of the week, and it suddenly struck me that the leaders were the one thing I had always skipped. Leaders! How were they written? what were they about? My mother was already sitting triumphant among my socks, and I durst not let her see me quaking. I retired to ponder, and presently she came to me with the daily paper. Which were the leaders? she wanted to know, so evidently I could get no help from her. Had she any more newspapers? I asked, and after rummaging she produced a few with which her boxes had been lined. Others, very dusty, came from beneath carpets, and lastly a sooty bundle was dragged down the chimney. Surrounded by these, I sat down and studied how to become a journalist.

CHAPTER IV

AN EDITOR

A DEVOUT lady, to whom some friend had presented one of my books, used to say when asked how she was getting on with it, "Sal, it's dreary, weary, uphill work, but I've wrastled through with tougher jobs in my time, and, please God, I'll wrastle through with this one." It was in this spirit, I fear, though she never told me so, that my mother wrestled for the next year or more with my leaders, and indeed I was always genuinely sorry for the people I saw reading them. In my spare hours I was trying journalism of another kind and sending it to London, but nearly eighteen months elapsed before there came to me, as unlooked for as a telegram, the thought that there was something quaint about my native place. A boy who found that a knife had been put into his pocket in the night could not have been more surprised. A few days afterwards I sent my mother a London evening paper with an article entitled "An Auld Licht Community," and they told me that when she saw the heading she laughed, because there was something droll to her in the sight of the words Auld Licht in print. For her, as for me, that newspaper was soon to have the face of a friend. To this day I never pass its placards in the street without shaking it by the hand, and she used to sew its pages together as lovingly as though they were a child's frock; but let the truth be told, when she read that first article she became alarmed, and fearing the talk of the town, hid the paper from all eyes. For some time afterwards, while I proudly pictured her showing this and similar articles to all who felt an interest in me, she was really concealing them fearfully in a bandbox on the garret stair. And she wanted to know by return of post whether I was paid for these articles just as I was paid for real articles; when she heard that I was paid better, she laughed again and had them out of the bandbox for re-reading, and it cannot be denied that she thought the London editor a fine fellow but slightly soft.

When I sent off that first sketch I thought I had exhausted the subject, but our editor wrote that he would like something more of the same, so I sent him a marriage, and he took it, and then I tried him with a funeral, and he took it, and really it began to look as if we had him. Now my mother might have been discovered, in answer to certain excited letters, flinging the bundle of undarned socks from her lap, and "going in for literature;" she was racking her brains, by request, for memories I might convert into articles, and they came to me in letters which she dictated to my sisters. How well I could hear her saying between the lines: "But the editor-man will never stand that, it's perfect blethers" —— "By this post it must go, I tell you; we must take the editor when he's hungry — we canna be blamed for it, can we? he prints them of his free will, so the wite is his" —— "But I'm near terrified.—If London folk reads them we're done for." And I was sounded as to the advisability of sending him a present of a lippie of short-bread, which was to be her crafty way of getting round him. By this time, though my mother and I were hundreds of miles apart, you may picture us waving our hands to each other across country, and shouting "Hurrah!" You may also picture the editor in his office thinking he was behaving like a shrewd man of business, and unconscious that up in the north there was an elderly lady chuckling so much at him that she could scarcely scrape the potatoes.

I was now able to see my mother again, and the park seats no longer loomed so prominent in our map of London. Still, there they were, and it was with an effort that she summoned up courage to let me go. She feared changes, and who could tell that the editor would continue to be kind? Perhaps when he saw me —

She seemed to be very much afraid of his seeing

me, and this, I would point out, was a reflection on my appearance or my manner.

No, what she meant was that I looked so young, and—and that would take him aback, for had I not written as an aged man?

"But he knows my age, mother."

"I'm glad of that, but maybe he wouldna like you when he saw you."

"Oh, it is my manner, then!"

"I dinna say that, but ——"

Here my sister would break in: "The short and the long of it is just this, she thinks nobody has such manners as herself. Can you deny it, you vain woman?"

My mother would deny it vigorously.

"You stand there," my sister would say with affected scorn, "and tell me you don't think you could get the better of that man quicker than any of us?"

"Sal, I'm thinking I could manage him," says my mother, with a chuckle.

"How would you set about it?"

Then my mother would begin to laugh. "I would find out first if he had a family, and then I would say they were the finest family in London."

"Yes, that is just what you would do, you cunning woman! But if he has no family?"

"I would say what great men editors are!"

"He would see through you."

"Not he!"

"You don't understand that what imposes on common folk would never hoodwink an editor."

"That's where you are wrong. Gentle or simple, stupid or clever, the men are all alike in the hands of a woman that flatters them."

"Ah, I'm sure there are better ways of getting round an editor than that."

"I daresay there are," my mother would say with conviction, "but if you try that plan you will never need to try another."

"How artful you are, mother — you with your soft face! Do you not think shame?"

"Pooh!" says my mother brazenly.

"I can see the reason why you are so popular with men."

"Ay, you can see it, but they never will."

"Well, how would you dress yourself if you were going to that editor's office?"

"Of course I would wear my silk and my Sabbath bonnet."

"It is you who are shortsighted now, mother. I tell you, you would manage him better if you just put on your old grey shawl and one of your bonny white mutches, and went in half smiling and half timid and said, 'I am the mother of him that writes about the Auld Lichts, and I want you to promise that he will never have to sleep in the open air.'"

But my mother would shake her head at this,

and reply almost hotly, "I tell you if I ever go into that man's office, I go in silk."

I wrote and asked the editor if I should come to London, and he said No, so I went, laden with charges from my mother to walk in the middle of the street (they jump out on you as you are turning a corner), never to venture forth after sunset, and always to lock up everything (I who could never lock up anything, except my heart in company). Thanks to this editor, for the others would have nothing to say to me though I battered on all their doors, she was soon able to sleep at nights without the dread that I should be waking presently with the iron-work of certain seats figured on my person, and what relieved her very much was that I had begun to write as if Auld Lichts were not the only people I knew of. So long as I confined myself to them she had a haunting fear that, even though the editor remained blind to his best interests, something would one day go crack within me (as the mainspring of a watch breaks) and my pen refuse to write for evermore. "Ay, I like the article brawly," she would say timidly, "but I'm doubting it's the last — I always have a sort of terror the new one may be the last," and if many days elapsed before the arrival of another article her face would say mournfully, "The blow has fallen—he can think of nothing more to write about." If I ever shared her fears I never told her

so, and the articles that were not Scotch grew in
number until there were hundreds of them, all
carefully preserved by her: they were the only
thing in the house that, having served one purpose, she did not convert into something else, yet
they could give her uneasy moments. This was
because I nearly always assumed a character when
I wrote; I must be a country squire, or an undergraduate, or a butler, or a member of the House
of Lords, or a dowager, or a lady called Sweet
Seventeen, or an engineer in India, else was my
pen clogged; and though this gave my mother
certain fearful joys, causing her to laugh unexpectedly (so far as my articles were concerned she
nearly always laughed in the wrong place), it also
scared her. Much to her amusement, the editor
continued to prefer the Auld Licht papers, however, as was proved (to those who knew him) by
his way of thinking that the others would pass as
they were, while he sent these back and asked me
to make them better. Here again she came to
my aid. I had said that the row of stockings were
hung on a string by the fire, which was a recollec-
tion of my own, but she could tell me whether
they were hung upside down. She became quite
skilful at sending or giving me (for now I could
be with her half the year) the right details, but
still she smiled at the editor, and in her gay moods
she would say, " I was fifteen when I got my first

pair of elastic-sided boots. Tell him my charge for this important news is two pounds ten."

"Ay, but though we're doing well, it's no the same as if they were a book with your name on it." So the ambitious woman would say with a sigh, and I did my best to turn the Auld Licht sketches into a book with my name on it. Then perhaps we understood most fully how good a friend our editor had been, for just as I had been able to find no well-known magazine — and I think I tried all — which would print any article or story about the poor of my native land, so now the publishers, Scotch and English, refused to accept the book as a gift. I was willing to present it to them, but they would have it in no guise; there seemed to be a blight on everything that was Scotch. I daresay we sighed, but never were collaborators more prepared for rejection, and though my mother might look wistfully at the scorned manuscript at times and murmur, "You poor cold little crittur shut away in a drawer, are you dead or just sleeping?" she had still her editor to say grace over. And at last publishers, sufficiently daring and far more than sufficiently generous, were found for us by a dear friend, who made one woman very "uplifted." He also was an editor, and had as large a part in making me a writer of books as the other in determining what the books should be about.

AN EDITOR

Now that I was an author, I must get into a club. But you should have heard my mother on clubs! She knew of none save those to which you subscribe a pittance weekly in anticipation of rainy days, and the London clubs were her scorn. Often I heard her on them — she raised her voice to make me hear, whichever room I might be in, and it was when she was sarcastic that I skulked the most: "Thirty pounds is what he will have to pay the first year, and ten pounds a year after that. You think it's a lot o' siller? Oh, no, you're mista'en — it's nothing ava. For the third part of thirty pounds you could rent a four-roomed house, but what is a four-roomed house, what is thirty pounds, compared to the glory of being a member of a club! Where does the glory come in? Sal, you needna ask me, I'm just a doited auld stock that never set foot in a club, so it's little I ken about glory. But I may tell you if you bide in London and canna become member of a club, the best you can do is to tie a rope round your neck and slip out of the world. What use are they? Oh, they're terrible useful. You see, it doesna do for a man in London to eat his dinner in his lodgings. Other men shake their heads at him. He maun away to his club if he is to be respected. Does he get good dinners at the club? Oh, they cow! You get no common beef at clubs; there is a manzy of different things all

271

sauced up to be unlike themsels. Even the potatoes daurna look like potatoes. If the food in a
club looks like what it is, the members run about,
flinging up their hands and crying, ' Woe is me!'
Then this is another thing, you get your letters
sent to the club instead of to your lodgings. You
see, you would get them sooner at your lodgings,
and you may have to trudge weary miles to the
club for them; but that's a great advantage, and
cheap at thirty pounds, is it no? I wonder they
can do it at the price."

My wisest policy was to remain downstairs
when these withering blasts were blowing, but
probably I went up in self-defence.

" I never saw you so pugnacious before, mother."

" Oh," she would reply promptly, " you canna
expect me to be sharp in the uptake when I am
no a member of a club."

" But the difficulty is in becoming a member.
They are very particular about whom they elect,
and I daresay I shall not get in."

" Well, I'm but a poor crittur (not being member of a club), but I think I can tell you to make
your mind easy on that head. You'll get in, I'se
uphaud—and your thirty pounds will get in, too."

" If I get in, it will be because the editor is supporting me."

" It's the first ill thing I ever heard of him."

"You don't think he is to get any of the thirty pounds, do you?"

"'Deed if I did I should be better pleased, for he has been a good friend to us; but what maddens me is that every penny of it should go to those bare-faced scoundrels."

"What bare-faced scoundrels?"

"Them that have the club."

"But all the members have the club between them."

"Havers! I'm no to be catched with chaff."

"But don't you believe me?"

"I believe they've filled your head with their stories till you swallow whatever they tell you. If the place belongs to the members, why do they have to pay thirty pounds?"

"To keep it going."

"They dinna have to pay for their dinners, then?"

"Oh, yes, they have to pay extra for dinner."

"And a gey black price, I'm thinking."

"Well, five or six shillings."

"Is that all? Losh, it's nothing. I wonder they dinna raise the price."

Nevertheless my mother was of a sex that scorned prejudice, and, dropping sarcasm, she would at times cross-examine me as if her mind was not yet made up. "Tell me this, if you were to fall ill, would you be paid a weekly allowance out of the club?"

No, it was not that kind of club.

"I see. Well, I am just trying to find out what kind of club it is. Do you get anything out of it for accidents?"

Not a penny.

"Anything at New Year's time?"

Not so much as a goose.

"Is there any one mortal thing you get free out of that club?"

There was not one mortal thing.

"And thirty pounds is what you pay for this?"

If the committee elected me.

"How many are in the committee?"

About a dozen, I thought.

"A dozen! Ay, ay, that makes two pound ten apiece."

When I was elected I thought it wisdom to send my sister upstairs with the news. My mother was ironing, and made no comment, unless with the iron, which I could hear rattling more violently in its box. Presently I heard her laughing — at me undoubtedly, but she had recovered control over her face before she came downstairs to congratulate me sarcastically. This was grand news, she said without a twinkle, and I must write and thank the committee, the noble critturs. I saw behind her mask, and maintained a dignified

silence, but she would have another shot at me.
"And tell them," she said from the door, "you
were doubtful of being elected, but your auld
mother had aye a mighty confidence they would
snick you in." I heard her laughing softly as she
went up the stair, but though I had provided her
with a joke I knew she was burning to tell the
committee what she thought of them.

Money, you see, meant so much to her, though
even at her poorest she was the most cheerful
giver. In the old days, when the article arrived,
she did not read it at once, she first counted the
lines to discover what we should get for it — she
and the daughter who was so dear to her had calculated the payment per line, and I remember
once overhearing a discussion between them about
whether that sub-title meant another sixpence.
Yes, she knew the value of money; she had always in the end got the things she wanted, but
now she could get them more easily, and it turned
her simple life into a fairy tale. So often in those
days she went down suddenly upon her knees;
we would come upon her thus, and go away noise-
lessly. After her death I found that she had preserved in a little box, with a photograph of me as
a child, the envelopes which had contained my
first cheques. There was a little ribbon round
them.

CHAPTER V

I SHOULD like to call back a day of her life as it was at this time, when her spirit was as bright as ever and her hand as eager, but she was no longer able to do much work. It should not be difficult, for she repeated herself from day to day, and yet did it with a quaint unreasonableness that was ever yielding fresh delight. Our love for her was such that we could easily tell what she would do in given circumstances, but she had always a new way of doing it.

Well, with break of day she wakes and sits up in bed and is standing in the middle of the room. So nimble was she in the mornings (one of our troubles with her) that these three actions must be considered as one; she is on the floor before you have time to count them. She has strict orders not to rise until her fire is lit, and having broken them there is a demure elation on her face. The question is what to do before she is caught and hurried to bed again. Her fingers are tingling to prepare the breakfast; she would dearly love to

276

black-lead the grate, but that might rouse her
daughter from whose side she has slipped so cunningly. She catches sight of the screen at the foot
of the bed, and immediately her soft face becomes
very determined. To guard her from draughts
the screen had been brought here from the lordly
east room, where it was of no use whatever. But
in her opinion it was too beautiful for use; it be-
longed to the east room, where she could take
pleasant peeps at it; she had objected to its re-
moval, even become low-spirited. Now is her
opportunity. The screen is an unwieldy thing,
but still as a mouse she carries it, and they are
well under way when it strikes against the gas-
bracket in the passage. Next moment a reproachful hand arrests her. She is challenged with being
out of bed, she denies it — standing in the passage. Meekly or stubbornly she returns to bed,
and it is no satisfaction to you that you can say,
"Well, well, of all the women!" and so on, or
"Surely you knew that the screen was brought
here to protect you," for she will reply scornfully,
"Who was touching the screen?"

By this time I have awakened (I am through
the wall) and join them anxiously: so often has
my mother been taken ill in the night that the
slightest sound from her room rouses the house.
She is in bed again, looking as if she had never
been out of it, but I know her and listen sternly

to the tale of her misdoings. She is not contrite. Yes, maybe she did promise not to venture forth on the cold floors of daybreak, but she had risen for a moment only, and we just t'neaded her with our talk about draughts — there were no such things as draughts in her young days — and it is more than she can do (here she again attempts to rise, but we hold her down) to lie there and watch that beautiful screen being spoilt. I reply that the beauty of the screen has ever been its miserable defect: ho, there! for a knife with which to spoil its beauty and make the bedroom its fitting home. As there is no knife handy, my foot will do; I raise my foot, and then — she sees that it is bare, she cries to me excitedly to go back to bed lest I catch cold. For though, ever careless of herself, she will wander the house unshod, and tell us not to talk havers when we chide her, the sight of one of us similarly negligent rouses her anxiety at once. She is willing now to sign any vow if only I will take my bare feet back to bed, but probably she is soon after me in hers to make sure that I am nicely covered up.

It is scarcely six o'clock, and we have all promised to sleep for another hour, but in ten minutes she is sure that eight has struck (house disgraced), or that if it has not, something is wrong with the clock. Next moment she is captured on her way downstairs to wind up the clock. So evidently we must be up and doing, and as we have no servant, my sister disappears into the kitchen, having first asked me to see that "that woman" lies still, and "that woman" calls out that she always does lie still, so what are we blethering about?

She is up now, and dressed in her thick maroon wrapper; over her shoulders (lest she should stray despite our watchfulness) is a shawl, not placed there by her own hands, and on her head a delicious mutch. O, that I could sing the pæan of the white mutch (and the dirge of the elaborate black cap) from the day when she called witchcraft to her aid and made it out of snow-flakes, and the dear worn hands that washed it tenderly in a basin, and the starching of it, and the finger-iron for its exquisite frills that looked like curls of sugar, and the sweet bands with which it tied beneath the chin! The honoured snowy mutch, how I love to see it smiling to me from the doors and windows of the poor; it is always smiling — sometimes maybe a wavering, wistful smile, as if a tear-drop lay hidden among the frills. A hundred times I have taken the characterless cap from my mother's head and put the mutch in its place and tied the bands beneath her chin, while she protested but was well pleased. For in her heart she knew what suited her best, and would admit it, beaming, when I put a mirror into her hands and told her to look; but nevertheless the cap cost no less than so and so, whereas —— Was that a knock at the door? She is gone, to put on her cap!

She begins the day by the fireside with the New Testament in her hands, an old volume with its loose pages beautifully refixed, and its covers sewn and resewn by her, so that you would say it can never fall to pieces. It is mine now, and to me the black threads with which she stitched it are as part of the contents. Other books she read in the ordinary manner, but this one differently, her lips moving with each word as if she were reading aloud, and her face very solemn. The Testament lies open on her lap long after she has ceased to read, and the expression of her face has not changed.

I have seen her reading other books early in the day, but never without a guilty look on her face, for she thought reading was scarce respectable until night had come. She spends the forenoon in what she calls doing nothing, which may consist in stitching so hard that you would swear she was an over-worked seamstress at it for her life, or you will find her on a table with nails in her mouth, and anon she has to be chased from the garret (she has suddenly decided to change her curtains), or she is under the bed searching for bandboxes and asking sternly where we have put that bonnet. On the whole, she is behaving in a most exemplary way to-day (not once have we caught her trying

to go out into the washing-house), and we compliment her at dinner-time, partly because she deserves it, and partly to make her think herself so
good that she will eat something, just to maintain
her new character. I question whether one hour
of all her life was given to thoughts of food; in
her great days to eat seemed to her to be waste of
time, and afterwards she only ate to boast of it, as
something she had done to please us. She seldom
remembered whether she had dined, but always
presumed she had, and while she was telling me
in all good faith what the meal consisted of, it
might be brought in. When in London I had to
hear daily what she was eating, and perhaps she
had refused all dishes until they produced the pen
and ink. These were flourished before her, and
then she would say with a sigh, " Tell him I am to
eat an egg." But they were not so easily deceived;
they waited, pen in hand, until the egg was eaten.

She never " went for a walk " in her life. Many
long trudges she had as a girl when she carried
her father's dinner in a flaggon to the country
place where he was at work, but to walk with no
end save the good of your health seemed a very
droll proceeding to her. In her young days, she
was positive, no one had ever gone for a walk,
and she never lost the belief that it was an ab-
surdity introduced by a new generation with too
much time on their hands. That they enjoyed it

she could not believe; it was merely a form of showing off, and as they passed her window she would remark to herself with blasting satire, "Ay, Jeames, are you off for your walk?" and add fervently, "Rather you than me!" I was one of those who walked, and though she smiled, and might drop a sarcastic word when she saw me putting on my boots, it was she who had heated them in preparation for my going. The arrangement between us was that she should lie down until my return, and to ensure its being carried out I saw her in bed before I started; but with the bang of the door she would be at the window to watch me go: there is one spot on the road where a thousand times I have turned to wave my stick to her, while she nodded and smiled and kissed her hand to me. That kissing of the hand was the one English custom she had learned.

In an hour or so I return, and perhaps find her in bed, according to promise, but still I am suspicious. The way to her detection is circuitous.

"I'll need to be rising now," she says, with a yawn that may be genuine.

"How long have you been in bed?"

"You saw me go."

"And then I saw you at the window. Did you go straight back to bed?"

"Surely I had that much sense."

"The truth!"

"I might have taken a look at the clock first."

"It is a terrible thing to have a mother who prevaricates. Have you been lying down ever since I left?"

" Thereabout."

" What does that mean exactly?"

" Off and on."

" Have you been to the garret?"

" What should I do in the garret?"

" But have you?"

" I might just have looked up the garret stair."

"You have been redding up the garret again!"

"Not what you could call a redd up."

" O, woman, woman, I believe you have not been in bed at all!"

" You see me in it."

" My opinion is that you jumped into bed when you heard me open the door."

" Havers."

" Did you?"

" No."

" Well, then, when you heard me at the gate?"

" It might have been when I heard you at the gate."

As daylight goes she follows it with her sewing to the window, and gets another needleful out of it, as one may run after a departed visitor for a last word; but now the gas is lit, and no longer is it shameful to sit down to literature. If the book be a story by George Eliot or Mrs. Oliphant, her favourite (and mine) among women novelists, or if it be a Carlyle, and we move softly, she will read, entranced, for hours. Her delight in Carlyle was so well known that various good people would send her books that contained a page about him; she could place her finger on any passage wanted in the biography as promptly as though she were looking for some article in her own drawer, and given a date she was often able to tell you what they were doing in Cheyne Row that day. Carlyle, she decided, was not so much an ill man to live with as one who needed a deal of managing; but when I asked if she thought she could have managed him she only replied with a modest smile that meant " Oh, no! " but had the face of " Sal, I would have liked to try."

One lady lent her some scores of Carlyle letters that have never been published, and crabbed was the writing; but though my mother liked to have our letters read aloud to her, she read every one of these herself, and would quote from them in her talk. Side by side with the Carlyle letters, which show him in his most gracious light, were many from his wife to a friend, and in one of these a romantic adventure is described — I quote from memory, and it is a poor memory compared to my mother's, which registered everything by a method of her own: " What might be the age of

Bell Tibbits? Well, she was born the week I bought the boiler, so she'll be one-and-fifty (no less!) come Martinmas." Mrs. Carlyle had got into the train at a London station and was feeling very lonely, for the journey to Scotland lay before her and no one had come to see her off. Then, just as the train was starting, a man jumped into the carriage : to her regret until she saw his face, when, behold, they were old friends, and the last time they met (I forget how many years before) he had asked her to be his wife. He was very nice, and, if I remember aright, saw her to her journey's end, though he had intended to alight at some half-way place. I call this an adventure, and I am sure it seemed to my mother to be the most touching and memorable adventure that can come into a woman's life. "You see he hadna forgot," she would say proudly, as if this was a compliment in which all her sex could share, and on her old tender face shone some of the elation with which Mrs. Carlyle wrote that letter.

But there were times, she held, when Carlyle must have made his wife a glorious woman. "As when?" I might inquire.

"When she keeked in at his study door and said to herself, 'The whole world is ringing with his fame, and he is my man!'"

"And then," I might point out, "he would roar to her to shut the door."

MARGARET OGILVY

"Pooh," said my mother, "a man's roar is neither here nor there." But her verdict as a whole was, "I would rather have been his mother than his wife."

So we have got her into her chair with the Carlyles, and all is well. Furthermore, "to mak siccar," my father has taken the opposite side of the fireplace and is deep in the latest five columns of Gladstone, who is his Carlyle. He is to see that she does not slip away fired by a conviction, which suddenly over-rides her pages, that the kitchen is going to rack and ruin for want of her, and she is to recall him to himself should he put his foot in the fire and keep it there, forgetful of all save his hero's eloquence. (We were a family who needed a deal of watching.) She is not interested in what Mr. Gladstone has to say; indeed she could never be brought to look upon politics as of serious concern for grown folk (a class in which she scarcely included man), and she gratefully gave up reading "leaders" the day I ceased to write them. But like want of reasonableness, a love for having the last word, want of humour and the like, politics were in her opinion a mannish attribute to be tolerated, and Gladstone was the name of the something which makes all our sex such queer characters. She had a profound faith in him as an aid to conversation, and if there were silent men in the company would give him to them to talk

286

about, precisely as she divided a cake among children. And then, with a motherly smile, she would leave them to gorge on him. But in the idolising of Gladstone she recognised, nevertheless, a certain inevitability, and would no more have tried to contend with it than to sweep a shadow off the floor. Gladstone was, and there was an end of it in her practical philosophy. Nor did she accept him coldly; like a true woman she sympathised with those who suffered severely, and they knew it and took counsel of her in the hour of need. I remember one ardent Gladstonian who, as a general election drew near, was in sore straits indeed, for he disbelieved in Home Rule, and yet how could he vote against "Gladstone's man"? His distress was so real that it gave him a hang-dog appearance. He put his case gloomily before her, and until the day of the election she riddled him with sarcasm; I think he only went to her because he found a mournful enjoyment in seeing a false Gladstonian tortured.

It was all such plain sailing for him, she pointed out; he did not like this Home Rule, and therefore he must vote against it.

She put it pitiful clear, he replied with a groan.

But she was like another woman to him when he appeared before her on his way to the polling-booth.

"This is a watery Sabbath to you, I'm thinking," she said sympathetically, but without dropping her wires — for, Home Rule or no Home Rule, that stocking-foot must be turned before twelve o'clock.

A watery Sabbath means a doleful day, and "A watery Sabbath it is," he replied with feeling. A silence followed, broken only by the click of the wires. Now and again he would mutter, "Ay, well, I'll be going to vote — little did I think the day would come," and so on; but if he rose it was only to sit down again, and at last she crossed over to him and said softly (no sarcasm in her voice now), "Away with you, and vote for Gladstone's man!" He jumped up and made off without a word, but from the east window we watched him strutting down the brae. I laughed, but she said, "I'm no sure that it's a laughing matter," and afterwards, "I would have liked fine to be that Gladstone's mother."

It is nine o'clock now, a quarter past nine, half-past nine — all the same moment to me, for I am at a sentence that will not write. I know, though I can't hear, what my sister has gone upstairs to say to my mother:

"I was in at him at nine, and he said, 'In five minutes,' so I put the steak on the brander, but I've been in thrice since then, and every time he says, 'In five minutes,' and when I try to take the table-cover off, he presses his elbows hard on it, and growls. His supper will be completely spoilt."

"Oh, that weary writing!"

"I can do no more, mother, so you must come down and stop him."

"I have no power over him," my mother says, but she rises smiling, and presently she is opening my door.

"In five minutes!" I cry, but when I see that it is she I rise and put my arm round her. "What a full basket!" she says, looking at the waste-paper basket which contains most of my work of the night, and with a dear gesture she lifts up a torn page and kisses it. "Poor thing," she says to it, "and you would have liked so fine to be printed!" and she puts her hand over my desk to prevent my writing more.

"In the last five minutes," I begin, "one can often do more than in the first hour."

"Many a time I've said it in my young days," she says slowly.

"And proved it, too!" cries a voice from the door, the voice of one who was prouder of her even than I; it is true, and yet almost unbelievable, that any one could have been prouder of her than I.

"But those days are gone," my mother says solemnly, "gone to come back no more. You'll put by your work now, man, and have your supper, and then you'll come up and sit beside your mother for a whiley, for soon you'll be putting her away in the kirk-yard."

I hear such a little cry from near the door.

So my mother and I go up the stair together. "We have changed places," she says; "that was just how I used to help you up, but I'm the bairn now."

She brings out the Testament again; it was always lying within reach; it is the lock of hair she left me when she died. And when she has read for a long time she "gives me a look," as we say in the north, and I go out, to leave her alone with God. She had been but a child when her mother died, and so she fell early into the way of saying her prayers with no earthly listener. Often and often I have found her on her knees, but I always went softly away, closing the door. I never heard her pray, but I know very well how she prayed, and that, when that door was shut, there was not a day in God's sight between the worn woman and the little child.

CHAPTER VI

HER MAID OF ALL WORK

AND sometimes I was her maid of all work.

It is early morn, and my mother has come noise-lessly into my room. I know it is she, though my eyes are shut, and I am only half awake. Per-haps I was dreaming of her, for I accept her pres-ence without surprise, as if in the awakening I had but seen her go out at one door to come in at an-other. But she is speaking to herself.

"I'm sweer to waken him — I doubt he was working late — oh, that weary writing — no, I maunna waken him."

I start up. She is wringing her hands. "What is wrong?" I cry, but I know before she answers. My sister is down with one of the headaches against which even she cannot fight, and my mother, who bears physical pain as if it were a comrade, is most woe-begone when her daughter is the sufferer. "And she winna let me go down the stair to make a cup of tea for her," she groans.

"I will soon make the tea, mother."

"Will you?" she says eagerly. It is what she

has come to me for, but " It is a pity to rouse you," she says.

" And I will take charge of the house to-day, and light the fires and wash the dishes —— "

" Na, oh, no ; no, I couldna ask that of you, and you an author."

" It won't be the first time, mother, since I was an author."

" More like the fiftieth ! " she says almost glee-fully, so I have begun well, for to keep up her spirits is the great thing to-day.

Knock at the door. It is the baker. I take in the bread, looking so sternly at him that he dare not smile.

Knock at the door. It is the postman. (I hope he did not see that I had the lid of the kettle in my other hand.)

Furious knocking in a remote part. This means that the author is in the coal-cellar.

Anon I carry two breakfasts upstairs in triumph. I enter the bedroom like no mere humdrum son, but after the manner of the Glasgow waiter. I must say more about him. He had been my mother's one waiter, the only man-servant she ever came in contact with, and they had met in a Glasgow hotel which she was eager to see, having heard of the monstrous things, and conceived them to resemble country inns with another twelve bed-rooms. I remember how she beamed—yet tried

to look as if it was quite an ordinary experience—
when we alighted at the hotel door, but though she
said nothing I soon read disappointment in her face.
She knew how I was exulting in having her there,
so would not say a word to damp me, but I craftily drew it out of her. No, she was very comfortable, and the house was grand beyond speech,
but—but—where was he? he had not been very
hearty. "He" was the landlord; she had expected him to receive us at the door and ask if
we were in good health and how we had left the
others, and then she would have asked him if his
wife was well and how many children they had,
after which we should have all sat down together
to dinner. Two chambermaids came into her
room and prepared it without a single word to
her about her journey or on any other subject, and
when they had gone, "They are two haughty
misses," said my mother with spirit. But what
she most resented was the waiter with his swagger
black suit and short quick steps and the "towel"
over his arm. Without so much as a "Welcome
to Glasgow!" he showed us to our seats, not the
smallest acknowledgment of our kindness in giving such munificent orders did we draw from him,
he hovered around the table as if it would be un-
safe to leave us with his knives and forks (he
should have seen her knives and forks), when we
spoke to each other he affected not to hear, we

might laugh, but this uppish fellow would not join in, we retired, crushed, and he had the final impudence to open the door for us. But though this hurt my mother at the time, the humour of our experiences filled her on reflection, and in her own house she would describe them with unction, sometimes to those who had been in many hotels, often to others who had been in none, and whoever were her listeners she made them laugh, though not always at the same thing.

So now when I enter the bedroom with the tray, on my arm is that badge of pride, the towel; and I approach with prim steps to inform Madam that breakfast is ready, and she puts on the society manner and addresses me as " Sir," and asks with cruel sarcasm for what purpose (except to boast) I carry the towel, and I say, " Is there anything more I can do for Madam ? " and Madam replies that there is one more thing I can do, and that is, eat her breakfast for her. But of this I take no notice, for my object is to fire her with the spirit of the game, so that she eats unwittingly.

Now that I have washed up the breakfast things I should be at my writing, and I am anxious to be at it, as I have an idea in my head, which, if it is of any value, has almost certainly been put there by her. But dare I venture ? I know that the house has not been properly set going yet, there are beds to make, the exterior of the teapot is fair, but suppose some one were to look inside? What a pity I knocked over the flour-barrel! Can I hope that for once my mother will forget to inquire into these matters? Is my sister willing to let disorder reign until to-morrow? I determine to risk it. Perhaps I have been at work for half-an-hour when I hear movements overhead. One or other of them is wondering why the house is so quiet. I rattle the tongs, but even this does not satisfy them, so back into the desk go my papers, and now what you hear is not the scrape of a pen, but the rinsing of pots and pans, or I am making beds, and making them thoroughly, because after I am gone my mother will come (I know her) and look suspiciously beneath the coverlet.

The kitchen is now speckless, not an unwashed platter in sight, unless you look beneath the table. I feel that I have earned time for an hour's writing at last, and at it I go with vigour. One page, two pages, really I am making progress, when — was that a door opening? But I have my mother's light step on the brain, so I "yoke" again, and next moment she is beside me. She has not exactly left her room, she gives me to understand; but suddenly a conviction had come to her that I was writing without a warm mat at my feet. She carries one in her hands. Now that she is here, she remains for a time, and though she is in the armchair by the fire, where she sits bolt upright (she loved to have cushions on the unused chairs, but detested putting her back against them), and I am bent low over my desk, I know that contentment and pity are struggling for possession of her face : contentment wins when she surveys her room, pity when she looks at me. Every article of furniture, from the chairs that came into the world with me and have worn so much better, though I was new and they were second-hand, to the mantel-border of fashionable design which she sewed in her seventieth year, having picked up the stitch in half a lesson, has its story of fight and attainment for her, hence her satisfaction; but she sighs at sight of her son, dipping and tearing, and chewing the loathly pen.

"Oh, that weary writing!"

In vain do I tell her that writing is as pleasant to me as ever was the prospect of a tremendous day's ironing to her; that (to some, though not to me) new chapters are as easy to turn out as new bannocks. No, she maintains, for one bannock is the marrows of another, while chapters — and then, perhaps, her eyes twinkle, and says she saucily, "But, sal, you may be right, for sometimes your bannocks are as alike as mine!"

Or I may be roused from my writing by her cry that I am making strange faces again. It is my contemptible weakness that if I say a character smiled vacuously, I must smile vacuously;

if he frowns or leers, I frown or leer; if he is a coward or given to contortions, I cringe, or twist my legs until I have to stop writing to undo the knot. I bow with him, eat with him, and gnaw my moustache with him. If the character be a lady with an exquisite laugh, I suddenly terrify you by laughing exquisitely. One reads of the astounding versatility of an actor who is stout and lean on the same evening, but what is he to the novelist who is a dozen persons within the hour? Morally, I fear, we must deteriorate — but this is a subject I may wisely edge away from.

We always spoke to each other in broad Scotch (I think in it still), but now and again she would use a word that was new to me, or I might hear one of her contemporaries use it. Now is my opportunity to angle for its meaning. If I ask, boldly, what was that word she used just now, something like " bilbie " or " silvendy "? she blushes, and says she never said anything so common, or hoots, it is some auld-farrant word about which she can tell me nothing. But if in the course of conversation I remark casually, " Did he find bilbie ? " or " Was that quite silvendy ? " (though the sense of the question is vague to me) she falls into the trap, and the words explain themselves in her replies. Or maybe to-day she sees whither I am leading her, and such is her sensitiveness that she is quite hurt. The humour goes out of her face (to find bilbie in some more silvendy spot), and her reproachful eyes — but now I am on the arm of her chair, and we have made it up. Nevertheless, I shall get no more old-world Scotch out of her this forenoon, she weeds her talk determinedly, and it is as great a falling away as when the mutch gives place to the cap.

I am off for my afternoon walk, and she has promised to bar the door behind me and open it to none. When I return,—well, the door is still barred, but she is looking both furtive and elated. I should say that she is burning to tell me something, but cannot tell it without exposing herself. Has she opened the door, and if so, why? I don't ask, but I watch. It is she who is sly now:

"Have you been in the east room since you came in?" she asks with apparent indifference.

"No; why do you ask?"

"Oh, I just thought you might have looked in."

"Is there anything new there?"

"I dinna say there is, but—but just go and see."

"There can't be anything new if you kept the door barred," I say cleverly.

This crushes her for a moment; but her eagerness that I should see is greater than her fear. I set off for the east room, and she follows, affecting humility, but with triumph in her eye. How often those little scenes took place! I was never told of the new purchase, I was lured into its presence, and then she waited timidly for my start of surprise.

"Do you see it?" she says anxiously, and I see it, and hear it, for this time it is a bran-new wicker chair, of the kind that whisper to themselves for the first six months.

"A going-about body was selling them in a cart," my mother begins, and what followed presents itself to my eyes before she can utter another word. Ten minutes at the least did she stand at the door argybargying with that man. But it would be cruelty to scold a woman so uplifted.

"Fifteen shillings he wanted," she cries, "but what do you think I beat him down to?"

"Seven and sixpence?"

She clasps her hands with delight. "Four shillings, as I'm a living woman!" she crows: never was a woman fonder of a bargain.

I gaze at the purchase with the amazement expected of me, and the chair itself crinkles and shudders to hear what it went for (or is it merely chuckling at her?). "And the man said it cost himself five shillings," my mother continues exultantly. You would have thought her the hardest person had not a knock on the wall summoned us about this time to my sister's side. Though in bed, she has been listening, and this is what she has to say, in a voice that makes my mother very indignant, "You drive a bargain! I'm thinking ten shillings was nearer what you paid."

"Four shillings to a penny!" says my mother.

"I daresay," says my sister; "but after you paid him the money I heard you in the little bed-room press. What were you doing there?"

My mother winces. "I may have given him a present of an old top-coat," she falters. "He looked ill-happit. But that was after I made the bargain."

"Were there bairns in the cart?"

"There might have been a bit lassie in the cart."

"I thought as much. What did you give her? I heard you in the pantry."

"Four shillings was what I got that chair for," replies my mother firmly. If I don't interfere there will be a coldness between them for at least a minute. "There is blood on your finger," I say to my mother.

"So there is," she says, concealing her hand.

"Blood!" exclaims my sister anxiously, and then with a cry of triumph, "I warrant it's jelly. You gave that lassie one of the jelly-cans!"

The Glasgow waiter brings up tea, and presently my sister is able to rise, and after a sharp fight I am expelled from the kitchen. The last thing I do as maid of all work is to lug upstairs the clothes-basket which has just arrived with the mangling.

Now there is delicious linen for my mother to finger; there was always rapture on her face when the clothes-basket came in; it never failed to make her once more the active genius of the house. I may leave her now with her sheets and collars and napkins and fronts. Indeed, she probably orders me to go. A son is all very well, but suppose he were to tread on that counterpane!

My sister is but and I am ben — I mean she is in the east end and I am in the west — tuts, tuts, let us get at the English of this by striving: she is in the kitchen and I am at my desk in the parlour. I hope I may not be disturbed, for to-night I must make my hero say "Darling," and it needs both privacy and concentration. In a word, let me admit (though I should like to beat about the bush) that I have sat down to a love-chapter. Too long has it been avoided, Albert has called Marion "dear" only as yet (between you and me, these are not their real names), but though the public will probably read the word without blinking, it went off in my hands with a bang. They tell me — the Sassenach tell me — that in time I shall be able without a blush to make Albert say "darling," and even gather her up in his arms, but I begin to doubt it; the moment sees me as shy as ever; I still find it advisable to lock the door, and then — no witness save the dog — I "do" it dourly with my teeth clenched, while the dog retreats into the far corner and moans. The bolder Englishman (I am told) will write a love-chapter and then go out, quite coolly, to dinner, but such goings on are contrary to the Scotch nature; even the great novelists dared not. Conceive Mr. Stevenson left alone with a hero, a heroine, and a proposal impending (he does not know where to look). Sir Walter in the same circumstances gets out of the room by making his love-scenes take place between the end of one chapter and the beginning of the next, but he could afford to do anything, and the small fry must e'en to their task, moan the dog as he may. So I have yoked to mine when, enter my mother, looking wistful.

" I suppose you are terrible thrang," she says.

" Well, I am rather busy, but — what is it you want me to do ? "

" It would be a shame to ask you."

" Still, ask me."

" I am so terrified they may be filed."

" You want me to —— "

" If you would just come up, and help me to fold the sheets ! "

The sheets are folded and I return to Albert. I lock the door and at last I am bringing my hero forward nicely (my knee in the small of his back), when this startling question is shot by my sister through the keyhole:

" Where did you put the carrot-grater ? "

HER MAID OF ALL WORK

It will all have to be done over again if I let Albert go for a moment, so, gripping him hard, I shout indignantly that I have not seen the carrot-grater.

"Then what did you grate the carrots on?" asks the voice, and the door-handle is shaken just as I shake Albert.

"On a broken cup," I reply with surprising readiness, and I get to work again, but am less engrossed, for a conviction grows on me that I put the carrot-grater in the drawer of the sewing-machine.

I am wondering whether I should confess or brazen it out, when I hear my sister going hurriedly upstairs. I have a presentiment that she has gone to talk about me, and I basely open my door and listen.

"Just look at that, mother!"

"Is it a dish-cloth?"

"That's what it is now."

"Losh behears! it's one of the new table-napkins."

"That's what it was. He has been polishing the kitchen grate with it!"

(I remember!)

"Woe's me! That is what comes of his not letting me budge from this room. O, it is a watery Sabbath when men take to doing women's work!"

"It defies the face of clay, mother, to fathom what makes him so senseless."

" Oh, it's that weary writing."

" And the worst of it is, he will talk to-morrow as if he had done wonders."

" That's the way with the whole clanjamfray of them."

" Yes, but as usual you will humour him, mother."

" Oh, well, it pleases him, you see," says my mother, " and we can have our laugh when his door's shut."

" He is most terribly handless."

" He is all that, but, poor soul, he does his best."

CHAPTER VII

R. L. S.

THESE familiar initials are, I suppose, the best beloved in recent literature, certainly they are the
sweetest to me, but there was a time when my
mother could not abide them. She said "That
Stevenson man" with a sneer, and it was never
easy to her to sneer. At thought of him her face
would become almost hard, which seems incred-
ible, and she would knit her lips and fold her
arms, and reply with a stiff "oh" if you mentioned
his aggravating name. In the novels we have a
way of writing of our heroine, "she drew herself
up haughtily," and when mine draw themselves
up haughtily I see my mother thinking of Robert
Louis Stevenson. He knew her opinion of him,
and would write, "My ears tingled yesterday; I
sair doubt she has been miscalling me again."
But the more she miscalled him the more he delighted in her, and she was informed of this, and
at once said "The scoundrel!" If you would
know what was his unpardonable crime, it was
this, he wrote better books than mine.

I remember the day she found it out, which was not, however, the day she admitted it. That day, when I should have been at my work, she came upon me in the kitchen, " The Master of Ballantrae " beside me, but I was not reading: my head lay heavy on the table and to her anxious eyes, I doubt not, I was the picture of woe. " Not writing!" I echoed, no, I was not writing, I saw no use in ever trying to write again. And down, I suppose, went my head once more. She misunderstood, and thought the blow had fallen; I had awakened to the discovery, always dreaded by her, that I had written myself dry; I was no better than an empty ink-bottle. She wrung her hands, but indignation came to her with my explanation, which was that while R. L. S. was at it we others were only 'prentices cutting our fingers on his tools. " I could never thole his books," said my mother immediately, and indeed vindictively.

" You have not read any of them," I reminded her.

" And never will," said she with spirit.

And I have no doubt that she called him a dark character that very day. For weeks too, if not for months, she adhered to her determination not to read him, though I, having come to my senses and seen that there is a place for the 'prentice, was taking a pleasure, almost malicious, in

putting "The Master of Ballantrae" in her way.
I would place it on her table so that it said good-
morning to her when she rose. She would frown,
and, carrying it downstairs, as if she had it in
the tongs, replace it on its book-shelf. I would
wrap it up in the cover she had made for the latest
Carlyle: she would skin it contemptuously and
again bring it down. I would hide her spectacles
in it, and lay it on top of the clothes-basket and
prop it up invitingly open against her tea-pot.
And at last I got her, though I forget by which
of many contrivances. What I recall vividly is a
key-hole view, to which another member of the
family invited me. Then I saw my mother
wrapped up in "The Master of Ballantrae" and
muttering the music to herself, nodding her head
in approval, and taking a stealthy glance at the
foot of each page before she began at the top.
Nevertheless she had an ear for the door, for when
I bounced in she had been too clever for me;
there was no book to be seen, only an apron on
her lap and she was gazing out at the window.
Some such conversation as this followed:

"You have been sitting very quietly, mother."

"I always sit quietly, I never do anything, I'm
just a finished stocking."

"Have you been reading?"

"Do I ever read at this time of day?"

"What is that in your lap?"

"Just my apron."

"Is that a book beneath the apron?"

"It might be a book."

"Let me see."

"Go away with you to your work."

But I lifted the apron. "Why, it's 'The Master of Ballantrae!'" I exclaimed, shocked.

"So it is!" said my mother, equally surprised. But I looked sternly at her, and perhaps she blushed.

"Well, what do you think: not nearly equal to mine?" said I with humour.

"Nothing like them," she said determinedly.

"Not a bit," said I, though whether with a smile or a groan is immaterial; they would have meant the same thing. Should I put the book back on its shelf? I asked, and she replied that I could put it wherever I liked, for all she cared, so long as I took it out of her sight (the implication was that it had stolen on to her lap while she was looking out at the window). My behaviour may seem small, but I gave her a last chance, for I said that some people found it a book there was no putting down until they reached the last page.

"I'm no that kind," replied my mother.

Nevertheless our old game with the haver of a thing, as she called it, was continued, with this difference, that it was now she who carried the book covertly upstairs, and I who replaced it on the shelf, and several times we caught each other in the act, but not a word said either of us; we were grown self-conscious. Much of the play no doubt I forget, but one incident I remember clearly. She had come down to sit beside me while I wrote, and sometimes, when I looked up, her eye was not on me, but on the shelf where "The Master of Ballantrae" stood inviting her. Mr. Stevenson's books are not for the shelf, they are for the hand; even when you lay them down, let it be on the table for the next comer. Being the most sociable that man has penned in our time, they feel very lonely up there in a stately row. I think their eye is on you the moment you enter the room, and so you are drawn to look at them, and you take a volume down with the impulse that induces one to unchain the dog. And the result is not dissimilar, for in another moment you two are at play. Is there any other modern writer who gets round you in this way? Well, he had given my mother the look which in the ball-room means, "Ask me for this waltz," and she ettled to do it, but felt that her more dutiful course was to sit out the dance with this other less entertaining partner. I wrote on doggedly, but could hear the whispering.

"Am I to be a wall-flower?" asked James Durie reproachfully. (It must have been leap-year.)

"Speak lower," replied my mother, with an uneasy look at me.

"Pooh!" said James contemptuously, "that kail-runtle!"

"I winna have him miscalled," said my mother, frowning.

"I am done with him," said James (wiping his cane with his cambric handkerchief), and his sword clattered deliciously (I cannot think this was accidental), which made my mother sigh. Like the man he was, he followed up his advantage with a comparison that made me dip viciously.

"A prettier sound that," said he, clanking his sword again, "than the clack-clack of your young friend's shuttle."

"Whist!" cried my mother, who had seen me dip.

"Then give me your arm," said James, lowering his voice.

"I dare not," answered my mother. "He's so touchy about you."

"Come, come," he pressed her, "you are certain to do it sooner or later, so why not now?"

"Wait till he has gone for his walk," said my mother; "and, forby that, I'm ower old to dance with you."

"How old are you?" he inquired.

"You're gey an' pert!" cried my mother.

"Are you seventy?"

"Off and on," she admitted.

"Pooh," he said, "a mere girl!"

She replied instantly, "I 'm no to be catched with chaff;" but she smiled and rose, as if he had stretched out his hand and got her by the finger-tip.

After that they whispered so low (which they could do as they were now much nearer each other) that I could catch only one remark. It came from James, and seems to show the tenor of their whisperings, for his words were, "Easily enough, if you slip me beneath your shawl."

That is what she did, and furthermore she left the room guiltily, muttering something about redding up the drawers. I suppose I smiled wanly to myself, or conscience must have been nibbling at my mother, for in less than five minutes she was back, carrying her accomplice openly, and she thrust him with positive viciousness into the place where my Stevenson had lost a tooth (as the writer whom he most resembled would have said). And then like a good mother she took up one of her son's books and read it most determinedly. It had become a touching incident to me, and I remember how we there and then agreed upon a compromise: she was to read the enticing thing just to convince herself of its inferiority.

"The Master of Ballantrae" is not the best. Conceive the glory, which was my mother's, of knowing from a trustworthy source that there are at least three better awaiting you on the same shelf. She did not know Alan Breck yet, and he was as anxious to step down as Mr. Bally himself. John Silver was there, getting into his leg, so that she should not have to wait a moment, and roaring, " I'll lay to that !" when she told me consolingly that she could not thole pirate stories. Not to know these gentlemen, what is it like? It is like never having been in love. But they are in the house! That is like knowing that you will fall in love to-morrow morning. With one word, by drawing one mournful face, I could have got my mother to abjure the jam-shelf — nay, I might have managed it by merely saying that she had enjoyed " The Master of Ballantrae." For you must re- member that she only read it to persuade herself (and me) of its unworthiness, and that the reason she wanted to read the others was to get further proof. All this she made plain to me, eyeing me a little anxiously the while, and of course I accepted the explanation. Alan is the biggest child of them all, and I doubt not that she thought so, but curiously enough her views of him are among the things I have forgotten. But how enamoured she was of " Treasure Island," and how faithful she tried to be to me all the time she was reading it ! I had to put my hands over her eyes to let her know that I had entered the room, and even then she might try to read between my fingers, coming to herself presently, however, to say "It's a haver of a book."

"Those pirate stories are so uninteresting," I would reply without fear, for she was too engrossed to see through me. "Do you think you will finish this one?"

"I may as well go on with it since I have begun it," my mother says, so slily that my sister and I shake our heads at each other to imply, "Was there ever such a woman!"

"There are none of those one-legged scoundrels in my books," I say.

"Better without them," she replies promptly.

"I wonder, mother, what it is about the man that so infatuates the public?"

"He takes no hold of me," she insists. "I would a hantle rather read your books."

I offer obligingly to bring one of them to her, and now she looks at me suspiciously. "You surely believe I like yours best," she says with instant anxiety, and I soothe her by assurances, and retire advising her to read on, just to see if she can find out how he misleads the public. "Oh, I may take a look at it again by and by," she says indifferently, but nevertheless the probability is that as the door shuts the book opens, as if by some mechanical contrivance. I remember how she read "Treasure Island," holding it close to the ribs of the fire (because she could not spare a moment to rise and light the gas), and how, when bed-time came, and we coaxed, remonstrated, scolded, she said quite fiercely, clinging to the book, " I dinna lay my head on a pillow this night till I see how that laddie got out of the barrel."

After this, I think, he was as bewitching as the laddie in the barrel to her—Was he not always a laddie in the barrel himself, climbing in for apples while we all stood around, like gamins, waiting for a bite ? He was the spirit of boyhood tugging at the skirts of this old world of ours and compelling it to come back and play. And I suppose my mother felt this, as so many have felt it : like others, she was a little scared at first to find herself skipping again, with this masterful child at the rope, but soon she gave him her hand and set off with him for the meadow, not an apology between the two of them for the author left behind. But never to the end did she admit (in words) that he had a way with him which was beyond her son. "Silk and sacking, that is what we are," she was informed, to which she would reply obstinately, " Well, then, I prefer sacking."

" But if he had been your son ? "

" But he is not."

" You wish he were ? "

" I dinna deny but what I could have found room for him."

314

And still at times she would smear him with the name of black (to his delight when he learned the reason). That was when some podgy red-sealed blue-crossed letter arrived from Vailima, inviting me to journey thither. (His directions were, "You take the boat at San Francisco, and then my place is the second to the left.") Even London seemed to her to carry me so far away that I often took a week to the journey (the first six days in getting her used to the idea), and these letters terrified her. It was not the finger of Jim Hawkins she now saw beckoning me across the seas, it was John Silver, waving a crutch. Seldom, I believe, did I read straight through one of these Vailima letters; when in the middle I suddenly remembered who was upstairs and what she was probably doing, and I ran to her, three steps at a jump, to find her, lips pursed, hands folded, a picture of gloom.

"I have a letter from —— "

"So I have heard."

"Would you like to hear it?"

"No."

"Can you not abide him?"

"I canna thole him."

"Is he a black?"

"He is all that."

Well, Vailima was the one spot on earth I had any great craving to visit, but I think she always knew I would never leave her. Sometime, she said, she should like me to go, but not until she was laid away. "And how small I have grown this last winter. Look at my wrists. It canna be long now." No, I never thought of going, was never absent for a day from her without reluctance, and never walked so quickly as when I was going back. In the meantime that happened which put an end for ever to my scheme of travel. I shall never go up the Road of Loving Hearts now, on "a wonderful clear night of stars," to meet the man coming toward me on a horse. It is still a wonderful clear night of stars, but the road is empty. So I never saw the dear king of us all. But before he had written books he was in my part of the country with a fishing wand in his hand, and I like to think that I was the boy who met him that day by Queen Margaret's burn, where the rowans are, and busked a fly for him, and stood watching, while his lithe figure rose and fell as he cast and hinted back from the crystal waters of Noran-side.

CHAPTER VIII

A PANIC IN THE HOUSE

I was sitting at my desk in London when a telegram came announcing that my mother was again dangerously ill, and I seized my hat and hurried to the station. It is not a memory of one night only. A score of times, I am sure, I was called north thus suddenly, and reached our little town trembling, head out at railway-carriage window for a glance at a known face which would answer the question on mine. These illnesses came as regularly as the back-end of the year, but were less regular in going, and through them all, by night and by day, I see my sister moving so unwearyingly, so lovingly, though with failing strength, that I bow my head in reverence for her. She was wearing herself done. The doctor advised us to engage a nurse, but the mere word frightened my mother, and we got between her and the door, as if the woman was already on the stair. To have a strange woman in my mother's room — you who are used to them cannot conceive what it meant to us.

317

Then we must have a servant. This seemed only less horrible. My father turned up his sleeves and clutched the besom. I tossed aside my papers, and was ready to run the errands. He answered the door, I kept the fires going, he gave me a lesson in cooking, I showed him how to make beds, one of us wore an apron. It was not for long. I was led to my desk, the newspaper was put into my father's hand. "But a servant!" we cried, and would have fallen to again. "No servant comes into this house," said my sister quite fiercely, and, oh, but my mother was relieved to hear her. There were many such scenes, a year of them, I daresay, before we yielded.

I cannot say which of us felt it most. In London I was used to servants, and in moments of irritation would ring for them furiously, though doubtless my manner changed as they opened the door. I have even held my own with gentlemen in plush, giving one my hat, another my stick, and a third my coat, and all done with little more trouble than I should have expended in putting the three articles on the chair myself. But this bold deed, and other big things of the kind, I did that I might tell my mother of them afterwards, while I sat on the end of her bed, and her face beamed with astonishment and mirth.

From my earliest days I had seen servants. The manse had a servant, the bank had another;

one of their uses was to pounce upon, and carry away in stately manner, certain naughty boys who played with me. The banker did not seem really great to me, but his servant — oh, yes. Her boots cheeped all the way down the church aisle; it was common report that she had flesh every day for her dinner; instead of meeting her lover at the pump, she walked him into the country, and he returned with wild roses in his buttonhole, his hand up to hide them, and on his face the troubled look of those who know that if they take this lady they must give up drinking from the saucer for evermore. For the lovers were really common men until she gave them that glance over the shoulder which, I have noticed, is the fatal gift of servants.

According to legend we once had a servant — in my childhood I could show the mark of it on my forehead, and even point her out to other boys, though she was now merely a wife with a house of her own. But even while I boasted I doubted. Reduced to life-size she may have been but a woman who came in to help. I shall say no more about her lest some one comes forward to prove that she went home at night.

Never shall I forget my first servant. I was eight or nine, in velveteen, diamond socks ("Cross your legs when they look at you," my mother had said, "and put your thumb in your pocket and

leave the top of your handkerchief showing"),
and I had travelled by rail to visit a relative. He
had a servant, and as I was to be his guest she
must be my servant also for the time being—you
may be sure I had got my mother to put this
plainly before me ere I set off. My relative met
me at the station, but I wasted no time in hoping
I found him well. I did not even cross my legs
for him, so eager was I to hear whether she was
still there. A sister greeted me at the door, but I
chafed at having to be kissed; at once I made for
the kitchen, where, I knew, they reside, and there
she was, and I crossed my legs and put one thumb
in my pocket, and the handkerchief was showing.
Afterwards I stopped strangers on the highway
with an offer to show her to them through the
kitchen window, and I doubt not the first letter I
ever wrote told my mother what they are like
when they are so near that you can put your
fingers into them.

But now when we could have servants for ourselves I shrank from the thought. It would not
be the same house; we should have to dissem-
ble; I saw myself speaking English the long day
through. You only know the shell of a Scot until you have entered his home circle; in his office,
in clubs, at social gatherings where you and he
seem to be getting on so well he is really a house
with all the shutters closed and the door locked.

A PANIC IN THE HOUSE

He is not opaque of set purpose, often it is against his will — it is certainly against mine, I try to keep my shutters open and my foot in the door, but they will bang to. In many ways my mother was as reticent as myself, though her manners were as gracious as mine were rough (in vain, alas, all the honest oiling of them), and my sister was the most reserved of us all; you might at times see a light through one of my chinks: she was double-shuttered. Now, it seems to be a law of nature that we must show our true selves at some time, and as the Scot must do it at home, and squeeze a day into an hour, what follows is that there he is self-revealing in the superlative degree, the feelings so long dammed up overflow, and thus a Scotch family are probably better acquainted with each other, and more ignorant of the life outside their circle, than any other family in the world. And as knowledge is sympathy, the affection existing between them is almost painful in its intensity; they have not more to give than their neighbours, but it is bestowed upon a few instead of being distributed among many; they are reputed niggardly, but for family affection at least they pay in gold. In this, I believe, we shall find the true explanation why Scotch literature, since long before the days of Burns, has been so often inspired by the domestic hearth and has treated it with a passionate understanding.

Must a woman come into our house and discover that I was not such a dreary dog as I had the reputation of being? Was I to be seen at last with the veil of dourness lifted? My company voice is so low and unimpressive that my first remark is merely an intimation that I am about to speak (like the whirr of the clock before it strikes): must it be revealed that I had another voice, that there was one door I never opened without leaving my reserve on the mat? Ah, that room, must its secrets be disclosed? So joyous they were when my mother was well, no wonder we were merry. Again and again she had been given back to us; it was for the glorious to-day we thanked God; in our hearts we knew and in our prayers confessed that the fill of delight had been given us, whatever might befall. We had not to wait till all was over to know its value; my mother used to say, " We never understand how little we need in this world until we know the loss of it," and there can be few truer sayings, but during her last years we exulted daily in the possession of her as much as we can exult in her memory. No wonder, I say, that we were merry, but we liked to show it to God alone, and to Him only our agony during those many night-alarms, when lights flickered in the house and white faces were round my mother's bedside. Not for other eyes those long vigils when, night about, we sat watching, nor the awful nights when we stood together, teeth clenched — waiting — it must be now. And it was not then; her hand became cooler, her breathing more easy; she smiled to us. Once more I could work by snatches, and was glad, but what was the result to me compared to the joy of hearing that voice from the other room? There lay all the work I was ever proud of, the rest is but honest craftsmanship done to give her coal and food and softer pillows. My thousand letters that she so carefully preserved, always sleeping with the last beneath the sheet, where one was found when she died — they are the only writing of mine of which I shall ever boast. I would not there had been one less though I could have written an immortal book for it.

How my sister toiled — to prevent a stranger's getting any footing in the house! And how, with the same object, my mother strove to " do for herself" once more. She pretended that she was always well now, and concealed her ailments so craftily that we had to probe for them:

"I think you are not feeling well to-day?"

"I am perfectly well."

"Where is the pain?"

"I have no pain to speak of."

"Is it at your heart?"

"No."

"Is your breathing hurting you?"

" Not it."

" Do you feel those stounds in your head again ? "

" No, no, I tell you there is nothing the matter with me."

" Have you a pain in your side ? "

" Really, it's most provoking I canna put my hand to my side without your thinking I have a pain there."

" You have a pain in your side ! "

" I might have a pain in my side."

" And you are trying to hide it ! Is it very painful ? "

" It's — it's no so bad but what I can bear it."

Which of these two gave in first I cannot tell, though to me fell the duty of persuading them, for whichever she was she rebelled as soon as the other showed signs of yielding, so that sometimes I had two converts in the week, but never both on the same day. I would take them separately, and press the one to yield for the sake of the other, but they saw so easily through my artifice. My mother might go bravely to my sister and say, "I have been thinking it over, and I believe I would like a servant fine — once we got used to her."

" Did he tell you to say that ? " asks my sister sharply.

" I say it of my own free will."

" He put you up to it, I am sure, and he told

you not to let on that you did it to lighten my work."

" Maybe he did, but I think we should get one."

" Not for my sake," says my sister obstinately, and then my mother comes ben to me to say delightedly, " She winna listen to reason ! "

But at last a servant was engaged; we might be said to be at the window, gloomily waiting for her now, and it was with such words as these that we sought to comfort each other and ourselves:

" She will go early to her bed."

" She needna often be seen upstairs."

" We'll set her to the walking every day."

" There will be a many errands for her to run. We'll tell her to take her time over them."

" Three times she shall go to the kirk every Sabbath, and we'll egg her on to attending the lectures in the hall."

" She is sure to have friends in the town. We'll let her visit them often."

" If she dares to come into your room, mother ! "

" Mind this, every one of you, servant or no servant, I fold all the linen mysel."

" She shall not get cleaning out the east room."

" Nor putting my chest of drawers in order."

" Nor tidying up my manuscripts."

" I hope she's a reader, though. You could set her down with a book, and then close the door canny on her."

And so on. Was ever servant awaited so apprehensively? And then she came,—at an anxious time, too, when her worth could be put to the proof at once,—and from first to last she was a treasure. I know not what we should have done without her.

CHAPTER IX

MY HEROINE

WHEN it was known that I had begun another story my mother might ask what it was to be about this time.

"Fine we can guess who it is about," my sister would say pointedly.

"Maybe you can guess, but it is beyond me," says my mother, with the meekness of one who knows that she is a dull person.

My sister scorned her at such times. "What woman is in all his books?" she would demand.

"I'm sure I canna say," replies my mother determinedly. "I thought the women were different every time."

"Mother, I wonder you can be so audacious! Fine you know what woman I mean."

"How can I know? What woman is it? You should bear in mind that I hinna your cleverness" (they were constantly giving each other little knocks).

"I won't give you the satisfaction of saying her name. But this I will say, it is high time he was keeping her out of his books."

327

And then as usual my mother would give herself away unconsciously. "That is what I tell him," she says, chuckling, "and he tries to keep me out, but he canna; it's more than he can do!"

On an evening after my mother had gone to bed, the first chapter would be brought upstairs, and I read, sitting at the foot of the bed, while my sister watched to make my mother behave herself, and my father cried H'sh! when there were interruptions. All would go well at the start, the reflections were accepted with a little nod of the head, the descriptions of scenery as ruts on the road that must be got over at a walking pace (my mother did not care for scenery, and that is why there is so little of it in my books). But now I am reading too quickly, a little apprehensively, because I know that the next paragraph begins with — let us say with, "Along this path came a woman": I had intended to rush on here in a loud bullying voice, but "Along this path came a woman" I read, and stop. Did I hear a faint sound from the other end of the bed? Perhaps I did not; I may only have been listening for it, but I falter and look up. My sister and I look sternly at my mother. She bites her underlip and clutches the bed with both hands, really she is doing her best for me, but first comes a smothered gurgling sound, then her hold on herself relaxes and she shakes with mirth.

" That's a way to behave ! " cries my sister.

" I cannot help it," my mother gasps.

" And there's nothing to laugh at."

" It's that woman," my mother explains unnecessarily.

" Maybe she's not the woman you think her," I say, crushed.

" Maybe not," says my mother doubtfully. " What was her name ? "

" Her name," I answer with triumph, " was not Margaret; " but this makes her ripple again. " I have so many names nowadays," she mutters.

" H'sh ! " says my father, and the reading is resumed.

Perhaps the woman who came along the path was of tall and majestic figure, which should have shown my mother that I had contrived to start my train without her this time. But it did not.

" What are you laughing at now ? " says my sister severely. " Do you not hear that she was a tall, majestic woman ? "

" It's the first time I ever heard it said of her," replies my mother.

" But she is."

" Ke fy, havers ! "

" The book says it."

" There will be a many queer things in the book. What was she wearing ? "

I have not described her clothes. " That's a

mistake," says my mother. "When I come upon a woman in a book, the first thing I want to
know about her is whether she was good-looking,
and the second, how she was put on."

The woman on the path was eighteen years of
age, and of remarkable beauty.

"That settles you," says my sister.

"I was no beauty at eighteen," my mother ad-
mits, but here my father interferes unexpectedly.
"There wasna your like in this countryside at
eighteen," says he stoutly.

"Pooh!" says she, well pleased.

"Were you plain, then?" we ask.

"Sal," she replies briskly, "I was far from plain."

"H'sh!"

Perhaps in the next chapter this lady (or another)
appears in a carriage.

"I assure you we're mounting in the world," I
hear my mother murmur, but I hurry on without
looking up. The lady lives in a house where
there are footmen — but the footmen have come
on the scene too hurriedly. "This is more than
I can stand," gasps my mother, and just as she is
getting the better of a fit of laughter, "Footman,
give me a drink of water," she cries, and this sets
her off again. Often the readings had to end abruptly because her mirth brought on violent fits
of coughing.

Sometimes I read to my sister alone, and she

assured me that she could not see my mother among the women this time. This she said to humour me. Presently she would slip upstairs to announce triumphantly, " You are in again ! "

Or in the small hours I might make a confidant of my father, and when I had finished reading he would say thoughtfully, " That lassie is very natural. Some of the ways you say she had — your mother had them just the same. Did you ever notice what an extraordinary woman your mother is ? "

Then would I seek my mother for comfort. She was the more ready to give it because of her profound conviction that if I was found out — that is, if readers discovered how frequently and in how many guises she appeared in my books — the affair would become a public scandal.

" You see Jess is not really you," I begin inquiringly.

" Oh, no, she is another kind of woman altogether," my mother says, and then spoils the compliment by adding naïvely, " She had but two rooms and I have six."

I sigh. " Without counting the pantry, and it's a great big pantry," she mutters.

This was not the sort of difference I could greatly plume myself upon, and honesty would force me to say, " As far as that goes, there was a time when you had but two rooms yourself——"

· "That's long since," she breaks in. "I began with an up-the-stair, but I always had it in my mind — I never mentioned it, but there it was — to have the down-the-stair as well. Ay, and I've had it this many a year."

"Still, there is no denying that Jess had the same ambition."

"She had, but to her two-roomed house she had to stick all her born days. Was that like me?"

"No, but she wanted ——"

"She wanted, and I wanted, but I got and she didna. That's the difference betwixt her and me."

"If that is all the difference, it is little credit I can claim for having created her."

My mother sees that I need soothing. "That is far from being all the difference," she would say eagerly. "There's my silk, for instance. Though I say it mysel, there's not a better silk in the valley of Strathmore. Had Jess a silk of any kind — not to speak of a silk like that?"

"Well, she had no silk, but you remember how she got that cloak with beads."

"An eleven and a bit! Hoots, what was that to boast of! I tell you, every single yard of my silk cost ——"

"Mother, that is the very way Jess spoke about her cloak!"

She lets this pass, perhaps without hearing it, for solicitude about her silk has hurried her to the wardrobe where it hangs.

"Ah, mother, I am afraid that was very like Jess!"

"How could it be like her when she didna even have a wardrobe? I tell you what, if there had been a real Jess and she had boasted to me about her cloak with beads, I would have said to her in a careless sort of voice, 'Step across with me, Jess, and I'll let you see something that is hanging in my wardrobe.' That would have lowered her pride!"

"I don't believe that is what you would have done, mother."

Then a sweeter expression would come into her face. "No," she would say reflectively, "it's not."

"What would you have done? I think I know."

"You canna know. But I'm thinking I would have called to mind that she was a poor woman, and ailing, and terrible windy about her cloak, and I would just have said it was a beauty and that I wished I had one like it."

"Yes, I am certain that is what you would have done. But oh, mother, that is just how Jess would have acted if some poorer woman than she had shown her a new shawl."

"Maybe, but though I hadna boasted about my silk I would have wanted to do it."

"Just as Jess would have been fidgeting to show off her eleven and a bit!"

It seems advisable to jump to another book;

not to my first, because — well, as it was my first, there would naturally be something of my mother in it, and not to the second, as it was my first novel and not much esteemed even in our family. (But the little touches of my mother in it are not so bad.) Let us try the story about the minister.

My mother's first remark is decidedly damping. " Many a time in my young days," she says, " I played about the Auld Licht manse, but I little thought I should live to be the mistress of it ! "

" But Margaret is not you."

" N—no, oh no. She had a very different life from mine. I never let on to a soul that she is me ! "

" She was not meant to be you when I began. Mother, what a way you have of coming creeping in ! "

" You should keep better watch on yourself."

" Perhaps if I had called Margaret by some other name —— "

" I should have seen through her just the same. As soon as I heard she was the mother I began to laugh. In some ways, though, she's no so very like me. She was long in finding out about Babbie. I'se uphaud I should have been quicker."

"Babbie, you see, kept close to the garden wall."

" It's not the wall up at the manse that would have hidden her from me."

" She came out in the dark."

"I'm thinking she would have found me looking for her with a candle."

"And Gavin was secretive."

"That would have put me on my mettle."

"She never suspected anything."

"I wonder at her."

But my new heroine is to be a child. What
has madam to say to that?

A child! Yes, she has something to say even
to that. "This beats all!" are the words.

"Come, come, mother, I see what you are
thinking, but I assure you that this time ——"

"Of course not," she said soothingly, "oh, no,
she canna be me;" but anon her real thoughts are
revealed by the artless remark, "I doubt, though,
this is a tough job you have on hand — it is so
long since I was a bairn."

We came very close to each other in those
talks. "It is a queer thing," she would say softly,
"that near everything you write is about this bit
place. You little expected that when you began.
I mind well the time when it never entered your
head, any more than mine, that you could write a
page about our squares and wynds. I wonder
how it has come about?"

There was a time when I could not have answered that question, but that time had long
passed. "I suppose, mother, it was because you
were most at home in your own town, and there

was never much pleasure to me in writing of people who could not have known you, nor of squares and wynds you never passed through, nor of a countryside where you never carried your father's dinner in a flaggon. There is scarce a house in all my books where I have not seemed to see you a thousand times, bending over the fireplace or winding up the clock."

"And yet you used to be in such a quandary because you knew nobody you could make your women-folk out of! Do you mind that, and how we both laughed at the notion of your having to make them out of me?"

"I remember."

"And now you've gone back to my father's time. It's more than sixty years since I carried his dinner in a flaggon through the long parks of Kinnordy."

"I often go into the long parks, mother, and sit on the stile at the edge of the wood till I fancy I see a little girl coming toward me with a flaggon in her hand."

"Jumping the burn (I was once so proud of my jumps!) and swinging the flaggon round so quick that what was inside hadna time to fall out. I used to wear a magenta frock and a white pinafore. Did I ever tell you that?"

"Mother, the little girl in my story wears a magenta frock and a white pinafore."

"You minded that! But I'm thinking it wasna a lassie in a pinafore you saw in the long parks of Kinnordy, it was just a gey done auld woman."

"It was a lassie in a pinafore, mother, when she was far away, but when she came near it was a gey done auld woman."

"And a fell ugly one!"

"The most beautiful one I shall ever see."

"I wonder to hear you say it. Look at my wrinkled auld face."

"It is the sweetest face in all the world."

"See how the rings drop off my poor wasted finger."

"There will always be some one nigh, mother, to put them on again."

"Ay, will there! Well I know it. Do you mind how when you were but a bairn you used to say, 'Wait till I'm a man, and you'll never have a reason for greeting again?'"

I remembered.

"You used to come running into the house to say, 'There's a proud dame going down the Mary-wellbrae in a cloak that is black on one side and white on the other; wait till I'm a man, and you'll have one the very same.' And when I lay on gey hard beds you said, 'When I'm a man you'll lie on feathers.' You saw nothing bonny, you never heard of my setting my heart on anything, but what you flung up your head and cried,

337

'Wait till I'm a man.' You fair shamed me before the neighbours, and yet I was windy, too. And now it has all come true like a dream. I can call to mind not one little thing I ettled for in my lusty days that hasna been put into my hands in my auld age; I sit here useless, surrounded by the gratification of all my wishes and all my ambitions, and at times I'm near terrified, for it's as if God had mista'en me for some other woman."

"Your hopes and ambitions were so simple," I would say, but she did not like that. "They werena that simple," she would answer, flushing.

I am reluctant to leave those happy days, but the end must be faced, and as I write I seem to see my mother growing smaller and her face more wistful, and still she lingers with us, as if God had said, "Child of mine, your time has come, be not afraid," and she was not afraid, but still she lingered, and He waited, smiling. I never read any of that last book to her; when it was finished she was too heavy with years to follow a story. To me this was as if my book must go out cold into the world (like all that may come after it from me), and my sister, who took more thought for others and less for herself than any other human being I have known, saw this, and by some means unfathomable to a man coaxed my mother into being once again the woman she had been. On a day but three weeks before she died my father and I were called softly upstairs. My mother was sitting bolt upright, as she loved to sit, in her old chair by the window, with a manuscript in her hands. But she was looking about her without much understanding. "Just to please him," my sister whispered, and then in a low, trembling voice my mother began to read. I looked at my sister. Tears of woe were stealing down her face. Soon the reading became very slow and stopped. After a pause, "There was something you were to say to him," my sister reminded her. "Luck," muttered a voice as from the dead, "luck." And then the old smile came running to her face like a lamp-lighter, and she said to me, "I am ower far gone to read, but I'm thinking I am in it again!" My father put her Testament in her hands, and it fell open — as it always does — at the Fourteenth of John. She made an effort to read, but could not. Suddenly she stooped and kissed the broad page. "Will that do instead?" she asked.

CHAPTER X

FOR years I had been trying to prepare myself for my mother's death, trying to foresee how she would die, seeing myself when she was dead. Even then I knew it was a vain thing I did, but I am sure there was no morbidness in it. I hoped I should be with her at the end, not as the one she looked at last, but as him from whom she would turn only to look upon her best-beloved, not my arm but my sister's should be round her when she died, not my hand but my sister's should close her eyes. I knew that I might reach her too late; I saw myself open a door where there was none to greet me, and go up the old stair into the old room. But what I did not foresee was that which happened. I little thought it could come about that I should climb the old stair, and pass the door beyond which my mother lay dead, and enter another room first, and go on my knees there.

My mother's favourite paraphrase is one known in our house as David's because it was the last he

340

learned to repeat. It was also the last thing she read —

> Art thou afraid his power shall fail
> When comes thy evil day?
> And can an all-creating arm
> Grow weary or decay?

I heard her voice gain strength as she read it, I saw her timid face take courage, but when came my evil day, then at the dawning, alas for me, I was afraid.

In those last weeks, though we did not know it, my sister was dying on her feet. For many years she had been giving her life, a little bit at a time, for another year, another month, latterly for another day, of her mother, and now she was worn out. "I'll never leave you, mother."—"Fine I know you'll never leave me." I thought that cry so pathetic at the time, but I was not to know its full significance until it was only the echo of a cry. Looking at these two, then, it was to me as if my mother had set out for the new country, and my sister held her back. But I see with a clearer vision now. It is no longer the mother but the daughter who is in front, and she cries, "Mother, you are lingering so long at the end, I have ill waiting for you."

But she knew no more than we how it was to be; if she seemed weary when we met her on the stair, she was still the brightest, the most active

figure in my mother's room; she never complained, save when she had to depart on that walk
which separated them for half an hour. How reluctantly she put on her bonnet, how we had to
press her to it, and how often, having gone as far
as the door, she came back to stand by my mother's
side. Sometimes, as we watched from the window,
I could not but laugh, and yet with a pain at my
heart, to see her hasting doggedly onward, not an
eye for right or left, nothing in her head but the
return. There was always my father in the house,
than whom never was a more devoted husband,
and often there were others, one daughter in particular, but they scarce dared tend my mother —
this one snatched the cup jealously from their
hands. My mother liked it best from her. We
all knew this. "I like them fine, but I canna do
without you." My sister, so unselfish in all other
things, had an unwearying passion for parading it
before us. It was the rich reward of her life.

The others spoke among themselves of what
must come soon, and they had tears to help them,
but this daughter would not speak of it, and her
tears were ever slow to come. I knew that night
and day she was trying to get ready for a world
without her mother in it, but she must remain
dumb, none of us was so Scotch as she, she must
bear her agony alone—a tragic, solitary Scotch-
woman. Even my mother, who spoke so calmly to

us of the coming time, could not mention it to her. These two, the one in bed, and the other bending over her, could only look long at each other, until slowly the tears came to my sister's eyes, and then my mother would turn away her wet face. And still neither said a word, each knew so well what was in the other's thoughts, so eloquently they spoke in silence, " Mother, I am loath to let you go, and " Oh, my daughter, now that my time is near, I wish you werena quite so fond of me." But when the daughter had slipped away my mother would grip my hand and cry, " I leave her to you; you see how she has sown, it will depend on you how she is to reap." And I made promises, but I suppose neither of us saw that she had already reaped.

In the night my mother might waken and sit up in bed, confused by what she saw. While she slept, six decades or more had rolled back and she was again in her girlhood; suddenly recalled from it she was dizzy, as with the rush of the years. How had she come into this room ? When she went to bed last night, after preparing her father's supper, there had been a dresser at the window: what had become of the salt-bucket, the meal-tub, the hams that should be hanging from the rafters ? There were no rafters; it was a papered ceiling. She had often heard of open beds, but how came she to be lying in one ? To fathom these things she would try to spring out of bed, and be startled to find it a labour, as if she had been taken ill in the night. Hearing her move I might knock on the wall that separated us, this being a sign, prearranged between us, that I was near by, and so all was well, but sometimes the knocking seemed to belong to the past, and she would cry, " That is my father chapping at the door, I maun rise and let him in." She seemed to see him — and it was one much younger than herself that she saw — covered with snow, kicking clods of it from his boots, his hands swollen and chapped with sand and wet. Then I would hear — it was a common experience of the night — my sister soothing her lovingly, and turning up the light to show her where she was, helping her to the window to let her see that it was no night of snow, even humouring her by going downstairs, and opening the outer door, and calling into the darkness, " Is anybody there ? " and if that was not sufficient, she would swaddle my mother in wraps and take her through the rooms of the house, lighting them one by one, pointing out familiar objects, and so guiding her slowly through the sixty odd years she had jumped too quickly. And perhaps the end of it was that my mother came to my bedside and said wistfully, " Am I an auld woman ? "

But with daylight, even during the last week in which I saw her, she would be up and doing, for though pitifully frail she no longer suffered from any ailment. She seemed so well comparatively that I, having still the remnants of an illness to shake off, was to take a holiday in Switzerland, and then return for her, when we were all to go to the much-loved manse of her much-loved brother in the west country. So she had many preparations on her mind, and the morning was the time when she had any strength to carry them out. To leave her house had always been a month's work for her, it must be left in such perfect order, every corner visited and cleaned out, every chest probed to the bottom, the linen lifted out, examined and put back lovingly as if to make it lie more easily in her absence, shelves had to be repapered, a strenuous week devoted to the garret. Less exhaustively, but with much of the old exultation in her house, this was done for the last time, and then there was the bringing out of her own clothes, and the spreading of them upon the bed and the pleased fingering of them, and the consultations about which should be left behind. Ah, beautiful dream! I clung to it every morning; I would not look when my sister shook her head at it, but long before each day was done, I too knew that it could never be. It had come true many times, but never again. We two knew it, but when my mother, who must always be prepared so long beforehand, called for her trunk and band-boxes we brought them to her, and we stood silent, watching, while she packed.

The morning came when I was to go away. It had come a hundred times, when I was a boy, when I was an undergraduate, when I was a man, when she had seemed big and strong to me, when she was grown so little and it was I who put my arms round her. But always it was the same scene. I am not to write about it, of the parting and the turning back on the stair, and two people trying to smile, and the setting off again, and the cry that brought me back. Nor shall I say more of the silent figure in the background, always in the background, always near my mother. The last I saw of these two was from the gate. They were at the window which never passes from my eyes. I could not see my dear sister's face, for she was bending over my mother, pointing me out to her, and telling her to wave her hand and smile, because I liked it so. That action was an epitome of my sister's life.

I had been gone a fortnight when the telegram was put into my hands. I had got a letter from my sister, a few hours before, saying that all was well at home. The telegram said in five words that she had died suddenly the previous night. There was no mention of my mother, and I was three days' journey from home.

The news I got on reaching London was this:

my mother did not understand that her daughter was dead, and they were waiting for me to tell her.

I need not have been such a coward. This is how these two died — for, after all, I was too late by twelve hours to see my mother alive.

Their last night was almost gleeful. In the old days that hour before my mother's gas was lowered had so often been the happiest that my pen steals back to it again and again as I write: it was the time when my mother lay smiling in bed and we were gathered round her like children at play, our reticence scattered on the floor or tossed in sport from hand to hand, the author become so boisterous that in the pauses they were holding him in check by force. Rather woful had been some attempts latterly to renew those evenings, when my mother might be brought to the verge of them, as if some familiar echo called her, but where she was she did not clearly know, because the past was roaring in her ears like a great sea. But this night was the last gift to my sister. The joyousness of their voices drew the others in the house upstairs, where for more than an hour my mother was the center of a merry party and so clear of mental eye that they, who were at first cautious, abandoned themselves to the sport, and whatever they said, by way of humourous rally, she instantly

347

capped as of old, turning their darts against themselves until in self-defence they were three to one, and the three hard pressed. How my sister must have been rejoicing! Once again she could cry, " Was there ever such a woman!" They tell me that such a happiness was on the daughter's face that my mother commented on it, that having risen to go they sat down again, fascinated by the radiance of these two. And when eventually they went, the last words they heard were, " They are gone, you see, mother, but I am here, I will never leave you," and "Na, you winna leave me; fine I know that." For some time afterwards their voices could be heard from downstairs, but what they talked of is not known. And then came silence. Had I been at home I should have been in the room again several times, turning the handle of the door softly, releasing it so that it did not creak, and standing looking at them. It had been so a thousand times. But that night, would I have slipped out again, mind at rest, or should I have seen the change coming while they slept?

Let it be told in the fewest words. My sister awoke next morning with a headache. She had always been a martyr to headaches, but this one, like many another, seemed to be unusually severe. Nevertheless she rose and lit my mother's fire and brought up her breakfast, and then had to return to bed. She was not able to write her daily letter

to me, saying how my mother was, and almost the
last thing she did was to ask my father to write it,
and not to let on that she was ill, as it would distress me. The doctor was called, but she rapidly
became unconscious. In this state she was removed from my mother's bed to another. It was
discovered that she was suffering from an internal
disease. No one had guessed it. She herself
never knew. Nothing could be done. In this
unconsciousness she passed away, without knowing that she was leaving her mother. Had I
known, when I heard of her death, that she had
been saved that pain, surely I could have gone
home more bravely with the words,

> Art thou afraid his power shall fail
> When comes thy evil day ?

Ah, you would think so, I should have thought
so, but I know myself now. When I reached
London I did hear how my sister died, but still I
was afraid. I saw myself in my mother's room
telling her why the door of the next room was
locked, and I was afraid. God had done so much,
and yet I could not look confidently to Him for
the little that was left to do. "O ye of little faith!"
These are the words I seem to hear my mother
saying to me now, and she looks at me so sor-
rowfully.

He did it very easily, and it has ceased to seem

349

marvellous to me because it was so plainly His doing. My timid mother saw the one who was never to leave her carried unconscious from the room, and she did not break down. She who used to wring her hands if her daughter was gone for a moment never asked for her again, they were afraid to mention her name; an awe fell upon them. But I am sure they need not have been so anxious. There are mysteries in life and death, but this was not one of them. A child can understand what happened. God said that my sister must come first, but He put His hand on my mother's eyes at that moment and she was altered.

They told her that I was on my way home, and she said with a confident smile, " He will come as quick as trains can bring him." That is my reward, that is what I have got for my books. Everything I could do for her in this life I have done since I was a boy; I look back through the years and I cannot see the smallest thing left undone.

They were buried together on my mother's seventy-sixth birthday, though there had been three days between their deaths. On the last day, my mother insisted on rising from bed and going through the house. The arms that had so often helped her on that journey were now cold in death, but there were others only less loving, and she went slowly from room to room like one bidding good-bye, and in mine she said, " The beautiful rows upon rows of books, and he said every one of them was mine, all mine!" and in the east room, which was her greatest triumph, she said caressingly, "My nain bonny room!" All this time there seemed to be something that she wanted, but the one was dead who always knew what she wanted, and they produced many things at which she shook her head. They did not know then that she was dying, but they followed her through the house in some apprehension, and after she returned to bed they saw that she was becoming very weak. Once she said eagerly, "Is that you, David?" and again she thought she heard her father knocking the snow off his boots. Her desire for that which she could not name came back to her, and at last they saw that what she wanted was the old christening robe. It was brought to her, and she unfolded it with trembling, exultant hands, and when she had made sure that it was still of virgin fairness her old arms went round it adoringly, and upon her face there was the ineffable mysterious glow of motherhood. Suddenly she said, "Wha's bairn's dead? is a bairn of mine dead?" but those watching dared not speak, and then slowly as if with an effort of memory she repeated our names aloud in the order in which we were born. Only one, who should have come third among the ten, did she omit, the one in the next room, but at the end, after a pause, she said her name and repeated it again and again and again, lingering over it as if it were the most exquisite music and this her dying song. And yet it was a very commonplace name.

They knew now that she was dying. She told them to fold up the christening robe and almost sharply she watched them put it away, and then for some time she talked of the long lovely life that had been hers, and of Him to whom she owed it. She said good-bye to them all, and at last turned her face to the side where her best-beloved had lain, and for over an hour she prayed. They only caught the words now and again, and the last they heard were "God" and "love." I think God was smiling when He took her to Him, as He had so often smiled at her during those seventy-six years.

I saw her lying dead, and her face was beautiful and serene. But it was the other room I entered first, and it was by my sister's side that I fell upon my knees. The rounded completeness of a woman's life that was my mother's had not been for her. She would not have it at the price. "I'll never leave you, mother." — "Fine I know you'll never leave me." The fierce joy of loving too much, it is a terrible thing. My sister's mouth was firmly closed, as if she had got her way.

And now I am left without them, but I trust my memory will ever go back to those happy days, not to rush through them, but dallying here and there, even as my mother wanders through my books. And if I also live to a time when age must dim my mind and the past comes sweeping back like the shades of night over the bare road of the present, it will not, I believe, be my youth I shall see but hers, not a boy clinging to his mother's skirt and crying, " Wait till I'm a man, and you'll lie on feathers," but a little girl in a magenta frock and a white pinafore, who comes toward me through the long parks, singing to herself, and carrying her father's dinner in a flaggon.

THE DE VINNE PRESS